Life This Side of Heaven

Life This Side of Heaven

—— *Taking the Saviour to the Sand* ——

Richard Wenden

RESOURCE *Publications* · Eugene, Oregon

LIFE THIS SIDE OF HEAVEN
Taking the Saviour to the Sand

Resource Publications
An Imprint of Wipf and Stock Publishers
199 W. 8th Ave., Suite 3
Eugene, OR 97401

www.wipfandstock.com

PAPERBACK ISBN: 978-1-6667-8445-9
HARDCOVER ISBN: 978-1-6667-8446-6
EBOOK ISBN: 978-1-6667-8447-3

VERSION NUMBER 05/30/24

Dedication

To my family, and particularly my wife, Juliet, who supported me through this process. To think I started the DMin when our third child was only newly born—words don't do justice to how much I love you! To my supervisors—Dr. David Gustafson and Rev. Archie Poulos, whose insights have made this project better than I could have done on my own. I'm thankful for their pastoral care and encouragement. This project is also dedicated to the guys and girls of 'the Phoenix' (you know who you are) at St Andrew's Cronulla. Your desire to keep everyday mission on our agenda was a great encouragement. And finally to my brothers & sisters—the 'Saints' at Seaforth Anglican: my desire and longing is that our church will always spur one another on to consider how as 'aliens in exile' we can be that faithful presence wherever God has placed us.

Contents

List of Illustrations & Tables | x

Preface | xi

1 Introduction: Setting the Scene | 1
Surveying the Current Landscape: The challenges for churches in beachside suburbs in the Sydney metropolitan area 2
Why this Book? 5
The Task of this Book 5
What we will learn 7

2 The Decline of Christendom: From post-modern to post-Christian | 10
The 'No-Religion' Shift 17

3 Foundations: Mission, Exile & the Church | 23
The Mission of God and God's People 23
Exile in the Bible 26
The Return from Exile 27
1 Peter: Embracing Exile 28

4 Thinking about The Church and Its Mission | 47
What is church? 47
The Church's Task 51
Mission & Evangelism 53
The Church and the Kingdom of God 58

Models of Missional Thinking 61

    Incarnational 61

    The Atonement as Central (and a better model) 64

5 Sociological And Cultural Challenges | 69

Cronulla: A brief case study 70

Understanding Culture 73

    Christian Approaches to Culture 76

    Cultural Liturgies 79

Contextualisation: From Niebuhr to Keller 81

6 Attitudes & Aspirations: What the Research Revealed | 90

Methodological Considerations 90

Results 96

    'A' Church 96

    'P' Church 101

    'M2' Church 104

    'H' Church 109

    'M1' Church 113

    'W' Church 120

    'C' Church 123

    'N' Church 126

Community Gatekeepers 130

    Local Business Owner 130

    Community Organisation—Former President, Cronulla SLSC 133

    Local Councillor (and former Mayor) 137

What Can We Observe? 139

7 Where Do We Go from Here? | 146

Where do we go from here? 149

    Embracing an Urban Spirituality—recapturing the 'Nones' 149

    Reordering Disordered Loves 153

    Fostering a 'Faithful Presence' 164

Conclusion | 174

Appendix 1: Invitation to Participate in Interview | 177
Appendix 2: Consent for Participation in Interview Research | 179
Appendix 3: Survey & Interview Questions for Ministers | 181
Appendix 4: Community Interview Invitation Letter | 184
Appendix 5: Community 'Gatekeeper' Interview Questions | 185
Bibliography | 187

Illustrations & Tables

1. Average Adult Attendance in Sydney Anglican Coastal Churches 2000-2017 | 3

2. Average Adult Attendance for the Sydney Anglican Churches Interviewed | 4

3. No Religion by State & Territory, 2016 and 2021 | 17

4. An Example of Evangelism in our Local Churches | 116

Preface

FOR SOME YEARS NOW I've been fascinated by the intersection between church and culture: or more specifically church and the micro-cultures that make up beachside suburbs. My appointment as a Senior Minister to a church in a beachside suburb in the South of Sydney only heightened this interest when another minister remarked to me how difficult it had been for churches to break into that sphere. Over my 10 years of ministry at this church I discovered how he was right. I used to say to people when they asked me how church was going that quite often it was like "ploughing concrete". As I thought more about this and talked with colleagues, I also began to read the works of ministry practitioners and theologians who were thinking through areas of ministry like contextualization and interacting with the culture of our time. I realized a large part of the difficulty was due to the post-Christian context in which Churches in the 21st century find themselves. I discovered the ongoing challenge for ministry teams and their congregations was how to adapt to this changing landscape with the accompanying cultural shifts. Churches in suburban coastal contexts face many challenges, not the least of which is the lifestyle that comes with living in what are deemed to be 'destination' suburbs. This book started as a topic for a Doctor of Ministry dissertation in an attempt to consider these challenges afresh against the biblical and theological backdrop of the church's mission, in line with God's mission as outlined in Scripture. It explores these challenges through the lens of Scripture, alongside some broad Biblical Theological themes and first Peter in particular, to help God's people make sense of what it means to be 'aliens and strangers' in a 21st century Babylon of sorts.

The way to understand any culture in ministry is to get in amongst it. As I immersed myself in the culture of Cronulla through joining the local Surf Life Saving Club and as my family got involved in other school and community groups, we gained valuable insights into the cultural movements of the time and the geographical area. Doing this highlighted the importance of contextualisation as a way of being able to engage people with the gospel. My research and interviews which contributed to my dissertation showed how a shift in the church's thinking towards adopting a 'Third Place' posture enables us to show people what real gospel-oriented community looks like. Ultimately this book seeks to offer some ways forward along the lines of embracing an urban spirituality, helping people to see how the gospel can, in the words of James K. A. Smith 'reorder their disordered loves', as they are pointed towards Jesus, and how more intentional training in discipleship and evangelism might equip congregations to be a faithful presence in their spheres of influence.

It is my fervent hope and prayer that this book with its underlying methodological focus on congregations along Sydney's coastal fringe, will go some way to assisting churches that have historically struggled in coastal contexts to formulate strategies enabling them to be missionally effective, through a renewed approach to ministry planning. It is hoped this planning may bring significant, gospel-based, long-term impact on individual church members, the community life of the church, and therefore the lives of the unchurched/de-churched to bring blessing to their suburbs, growth to our churches, as we live life to God's glory this side of heaven.

Sydney, 2023

1

Introduction: Setting the Scene

ALL OF US CAN recall a moment in our lives when we have found ourselves in a place or situation that is outside our comfort zone. We can describe that as feeling like strangers in a strange land. This has been typified over again in popular culture whether by Marty McFly in *Back to the Future* trying to make sense of 1955; or Dorothy and her little dog Toto taking in the beauty and splendour of the land of Oz with Dorothy's famous words "Toto, I've a feeling we're not in Kansas anymore." My wife and I experienced our own 'strangers in a strange land' moment some years ago on our first trip to the United States. On our first morning in New York city trying to find a reasonable espresso (and coming up profoundly short)—as Aussies in New York we were definitely strangers in a strange land.

For Christians in the West in the 21st century, we are clearly not in Kansas anymore. In 2023, we are most definitely strangers in a strange land.

Part of the aim of this book is to explore the reasons behind this observation. Perhaps most notable is the climate in which the church finds itself: a post-Christian culture. The way in which the church seeks to adapt to these strange surroundings is a topic which continues to be covered (as well it should be). My desire is not so much to re-tread a well-trodden path, but more to utilize current thinking as a launchpad to explore further ways in which churches in suburban coastal contexts can be more effective in contextualisation, and thus engagement with their surrounds leading to more effective gospel proclamation to people, many of whom seemingly feel they have no need for the Christian gospel.

If only it were that easy, of course! For while much has been written to help church leaders to think in general terms about the areas mentioned above, the specifics of suburban coastal contexts which I will explore means that we are considering particular micro-cultures which have had a distinct impact on, and indeed have given a certain shape and flavour to Sydney's beachside suburbs.

This effect is, of course, not just limited to our culture; the church must shoulder some of the responsibility for this phenomenon. Traditionally, "church leaders as well as Christians in general have regarded the church as an institution to which outsiders must come in order to receive a certain product, namely, the gospel and all its associated benefits."[1] Indeed, for many churches, the term 'outreach' has become somewhat of a misnomer, with unbelievers/unchurched expected to come *in* to the church, rather than the church going *out* to them. As Frost and Hirsch put it, "the traditional church plants itself within a particular community, neighborhood, or locale and expects that people will come to it to meet God and find fellowship with others."[2] This type of missiology and ecclesiology is "attractional". Even the mega "seeker-sensitive" churches, using mall-marketing methodologies, have essentially 'attractional' ecclesiologies. Although innovative and contemporary to the culture, the focus is still on drawing people in to receive what the church has to offer, rather than going out and meeting people in their context.

Surveying the Current Landscape: The challenges for churches in beachside suburbs in the Sydney metropolitan area

Beachside suburbs in Sydney are generally highly affluent with a significant culture of secular hedonism. Some also experience highly transient populations, though as an example, the suburb in which the church was located where I served from 2010-2020 was less so compared to 8 years ago. A cursory look at the data from the 2016 census shows that Cronulla had a mix of young adults (i.e. university students, married or co-habiting couples) and young families living in units. One-quarter of those studying are tertiary students; in fact the 18-34 age bracket makes up a third of the

1. Frost and Hirsch, *Shaping of Things*, xi
2. Frost and Hirsch, *Shaping of Things*, 19

overall population of Cronulla. Of the 13,419 dwellings in Cronulla, 6,474 are unit/apartment dwellings. When it comes to those apartment dwellings, couples with no children make up 73%, while shared households of mainly young adults in units make up around 89%.[3]

These statistics reflect the gamut of micro-cultures. People move to the Sutherland Shire and are specifically drawn to Cronulla because of its culture and lifestyle. This migration has led over many decades to the establishment of different micro-cultures, the strongest being the surfing culture. As was established from interviews conducted with the 9 ministers in similar coastal contexts (chapter 6), people move in for a good time but not always a long time. This is because as we will see, many of these beachside suburbs are seen as the places to live: they are the destination and to be able to live there is often the ultimate goal. Area affordability however means that the 18-34 age bracket and young families are both examples of the transient nature of a suburb like Cronulla.

When it comes to religion in Cronulla, 28% indicated they had no religion, 59% indicated they had some Christian affiliation, and of that 59%, 30% identified themselves with the Anglican denomination. The question is, where are they? We know from data obtained from the Sydney Diocesan Registry that average church attendance in Sydney Anglican churches in a coastal context generally has largely plateaued since 2000, as the chart below shows.

AVERAGE ADULT ATTENDANCE IN SYDNEY ANGLICAN
COASTAL CHURCHES 2000-2017

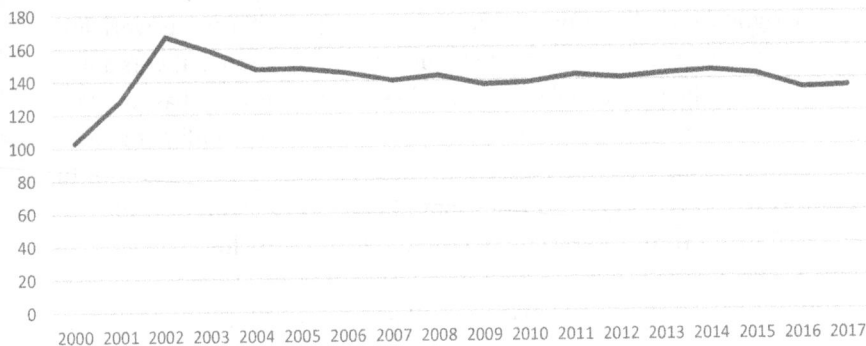

Average Adult Attendance in Sydney Anglican Coastal Churches 2000-2017

3. http://quickstats.censusdata.abs.gov.au/census_services/getproduct/census/2016/communityprofile/SSC11119?opendocument

Further, the next graph shows the growth and decline patterns for the Sydney Anglican Churches which participated in this research:

AVERAGE ADULT ATTENDANCES IN COASTAL CHURCHES INTERVIEWED

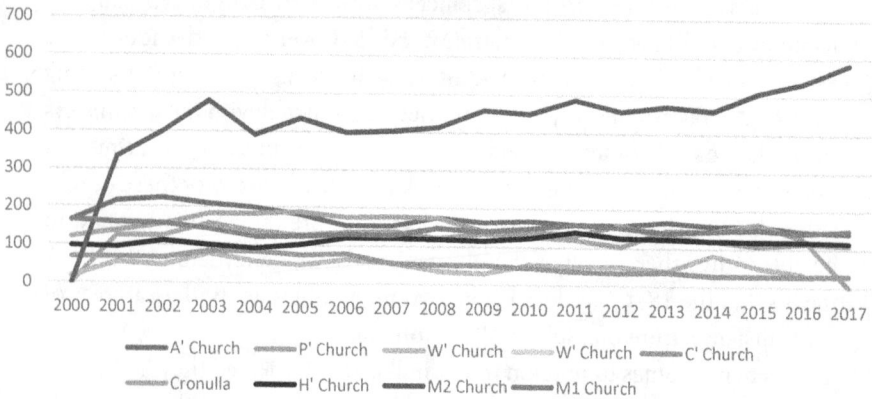

Average Adult Attendance for the Sydney Anglican Churches Interviewed, Including the Writer's Church

There are many reasons for this growth and decline, and these extend beyond the scope of this book. For our purposes, it is clear within this context that churches are finding they have to 'compete' with many extra-curricular and regular weekend activities. From Surf Life Saving Nippers and other Sunday sport, to a strong focus on getting the work-life balance right; from a 'time-poor' culture where often both parents work long hours outside the home, to a general malaise about church, there's a huge challenge in helping people see and believe that what Jesus has to offer is better. For beachside suburbs, it is my obversation that militant atheism is not the issue; people are generally happy to align themselves with the Anglican Church, as the statistics show. Instead, it is about the call of the gospel to cut through everything else which clamours for people's attention. Therefore, we need to become familiar with what makes people in this area "tick", so to speak. What are their hopes and dreams? What are their perceptions of church? Why don't they think they need Jesus and indeed fellowship within his church? These and other questions will be explored in an effort to help us understand the barriers to gospel growth among Sydney's beachside suburban churches.

Why this Book?

My journey in this research and writing this book was borne out of my pastoral desire to see our church fulfil the core business of any church—making disciples. At the time of undertaking this research I was serving as the Senior Minister (or Rector) in full-time ministry in the Parish of Cronulla, a now 'gentrified' suburb in the Sutherland Shire of Sydney, New South Wales, that is located right on the beach. I now serve in another coastal context as the Senior Minister in a church on Sydney's Northern Beaches.

Like many Sydney Anglican churches, St Andrew's Cronulla is a church whose ministry and infrastructure carries with it 'Christendom assumptions'. Situated on a block of land on the main road that takes you right into the suburb, the church remains one of the most iconic buildings in Cronulla, and probably the Sutherland Shire. Nicknamed 'The Elephant House' because of its once-striking resemblance to the elephant house enclosure at Taronga Zoo, St Andrew's, resplendent with its Byzantine architecture, including a magnificent dome, is an edifice that was designed to exercise Christendom functions in a Christendom context. Today most people walk past the church as they head to the beach or the local café, unsure of what denomination the church even is. Though located in a reasonably prominent position in Cronulla, St Andrew's and all it stands for is culturally very much on the fringes of people's minds, except for a handful of people. This church and its ministry team are working hard, struggling to try to understand its identity and mission in this post-Christian context. The temptation is to lean on methodologies that harken back to its once glorious (and not so ancient) past. The challenge is to develop a mission and strategy to reach post-Christian Cronulla where everything else is 'more appealing', for Cronulla is to many people 'God's country', or even 'heaven on earth'.

The Task of this Book

The scope of this book will assess the particular challenges or difficulties that churches face as they seek to reach the unchurched in beachside suburbs in Sydney and the Northern Illawarra. We will identify and explore the hurdles that make it harder for churches to reach the average non-Christian population that generally seems to have a notional interest in God and matters of faith, and how to change that so we might have an impact for God's Kingdom on these suburbs in this present cultural context.

I have focused mainly on Anglican churches for two reasons. First, my experience over 13 years as a Senior Minister of two Anglican churches in suburban coastal contexts in Sydney has given me many insights into the micro-culture. Second, the Anglican "brand" in Sydney being the more dominant "brand" among the Protestant churches is the most embedded in the concepts of "Christendom". Further as opposed to some denominations and newer 'Church Plants' because it has inherited concepts of Christendom which carries many obsolete assumptions from its inception in the colonial era into the present, there is much to gain from a shift in this mindset. At the same time, it is fair to assume that Sydney Anglicanism may be representative of other Protestant churches throughout Australia. There is certainly diversity in the history and traditions among the Protestant denominations, and while the flavour and traditions across the states of Australia are distinctive, there's enough common ground that insights gained can be applied to a broader context.

For a task this size, I considered various cultural aspects that have been, and continue to be, at play. Thus, a synthesising treatment of post-Christendom and what our post-Christian culture along Sydney's beaches looks like, is coupled with extensive theologically and biblically based reflection as to how churches ought to adjust to this reality. We also survey theological topics such as the doctrine of "church", what "exile" looks like in the 21st century; and what being "missional" as opposed to "attractional" looks like in this context.

Attention is also given to examining relevant Bible passages that relate to the church and its mission, the role of disciple-making, as well as what it looks like for God's people living as strangers in a strange land.

A qualitative approach to this research was undertaken to understand other beachside churches in their contexts. As well as acquiring and assessing the relevant data concerning Anglican church attendance since 2001, interviews were conducted with Senior Ministers of Anglican churches. A mix of churches (including a Baptist congregation) that are ministering effectively in their context as well those seemingly struggling will be considered as a way of assessing whether one aspect (among others) of the difficulties some churches face is a failure to have taken into account widespread demographic changes. Ten churches in close proximity to the beach and those with active Surf Life Saving Clubs were surveyed.

Interviews were also conducted with significant people in my "parish" community at the time to survey what they understand Christianity to be; what role (if any) it ought to play in their life; their perceptions of church in the 21st century, and what (if anything) would make them more interested and feel invested in the life of a church. This will be evaluated through the grid of a biblical-theological worldview from the perspective of an Evangelical Anglican pastor in Sydney Diocese.

The scope was limited to a largely urban context. I only sought to interview current Senior Ministers/Pastors, mainly from the mainstream Anglican denomination.

The questions asked of each of these Pastors were reflective of a snapshot in time. The research was designed recognising there have of course been significant changes both within the churches and the communities in which they're located (e.g., church attendance; demographic shifts and suburban growth to name a couple). Thus, the aim was to capture a picture of this moment in time of what churches have done/are doing in their current situation so that they might be better equipped for reaching their specific contexts. To aid this and provide a fuller picture, interviews were conducted with what I have called 'community gatekeepers' from the writer's suburb. These interviews looked at "what is" with the words of those who have some sort of influence or long-standing within the community. I also looked deeply at the setting of Cronulla as a typical beachside suburb and used the results to universalize to some extent recognising that there are always sociological nuances. This is what researchers call a "phenomenological approach" whereby I seek to justify that Cronulla is by and large typical of other beachside suburbs and that the findings therefore can legitimately be applied to churches in other coastal contexts.

What we will learn

It is my hope that in investigating how the landscape of suburban coastal centres in the Sydney Metropolitan and Northern Illawarra has shifted since the end of the modern era, this book will be able to show the impact of these changes on the churches in these areas, and how Christian churches have tried to respond to these shifts. I also hope to develop a picture of the complexities facing these churches based on multiple perspectives.[4] In

---

4. Creswell, *Research Design*, 186.

the final chapter, I suggest some strategies for churches seeking to relate meaningfully with the culture of these areas.

My hope is that a sustained concentration on how our past has shaped our present understanding of foundational theological issues relating to ecclesiology and mission will enable us to understand better the changing landscape: one that is most certainly post-Christian, meaning that the very memory of the gospel is dim. It's what we are left with as our culture has sought more and more to abandon the Christian worldview.[5] We will draw upon the way this has shaped urban Sydney and its people's thinking. A proper understanding of contextualisation through the lens by which we view the post-Christendom landscape, coupled with how we have histori- cally and theologically dealt with the question of the church and its relation to culture, will enable us to show people's baseline "cultural narratives" (the stories people tell to make sense of their shared existence) of their society and that the hopes of their hearts can only find resolution and fulfilment in Jesus[6]. It is my expectation that, by understanding significant shifts in our society and by developing a robust understanding of contextualisation, we can begin to help people (re)discover something about Christianity that is authentic, transcendent, and real, thus communicating to the unchurched in these suburban contexts the truth, beauty and liveability of the gospel. I am hoping that a critical exploration of past methods and a good self- understanding of our mission will enable anyone who reads this book to explore what the effective proclamation of the gospel in the community could look like for churches in their particular context.

A further outcome, shaped by qualitative analysis of interviews and observation of what different churches have done or are doing in their con- text, enabled us to explore a range of issues, i.e.,

- How well/poorly churches have adapted to the changing Sydney landscape;

- What ministries have been tried to reach the unchurched of their community;

- What churches have done or are doing to facilitate a shift in the mind- set of their members from attractional to missional;

- The approaches and strategies that thriving and struggling Christian churches have used to connect with their communities;

5. Veith, *Post Christian*, 18.
6. Keller, *Centre Church*, 90.

- To what extent a sustained cultural exegesis through demographic studies played a role in seeing the church having a positive and significant impact in the life of their suburb.

My hope in the end is that this will enable us to explore pathways that may assist churches struggling in their particular urban context, to move from an attractional mode of thinking about ministry and church life to a mindset that enables them to carry out effective gospel ministry to their community and underlying sub-cultures. I hope this book will be a help for churches that perhaps have historically struggled to be missionally-focused, serving as an encouragement in reconsidering their approach to ministry planning. Furthermore, it is hoped that this planning may bring significant, gospel-based, long-term impact on individual church members, the community life of the church and therefore the lives of the unchurched/de-churched to bring blessing to their suburbs, growth to the respective churches, and glory to God.

2

The Decline of Christendom: From post-modern to post-Christian

MUCH OF WHAT WE do and who we are as the local church has been shaped by the concept of "Christendom". Even though we live in a post-Christendom era, the habits and assumptions of Christendom continue to influence our practice of evangelism, our view of church and our understanding of the relationship between church and culture. The subsequent collapse of Christendom has not only located the church in a new place, but it also raises fundamental questions surrounding the church's identity and mission. To frame this positively, Christendom's collapse and all that comes with it, presents us with new opportunities to envisage the relationship between church and culture.

To understand our present position, the questions we face, and the assumptions we hold, we need to examine some of the aspects of Christendom and its impact on how the church understands its identity and its mission.

Following the Edict of Milan in AD313, the church experienced significant change in status and even legitimacy. As the church was officially accepted and Christianity became a politically and culturally established religion, people began to meet in specifically designated buildings where the professional clergy were in charge; and so the obligatory Sunday gatherings became the norm.

With external border pressures on the Roman Empire, a sharp distinction was made between what became known as "Christendom" and "heathendom". There was great emphasis placed on the latter and the need for those of heathendom to be converted. Steps taken to bring this about changed the nature of Christianity, for as the church expanded into non-Jewish communities, Christianity expanded at an exponential rate—and along with it issues of civil control.[1]

Darrell Guder contends that the gradual disintegration of the Roman Empire which led to migration and the changing of the cultural map in Europe meant that Christian mission was profoundly effective. Cultures became integrated into the Christian civilisation over which, in the West, the Roman pope exercised authority[2].

Throughout the Middle Ages and right into the Renaissance, Christendom flourished with a strong alliance between church and state. Church and politics were intertwined with the assumption that Christian values undergirded society.[3]

Along with various political, social, and economic shifts, and finding itself in a predominantly Christian culture, the church lost its distinctiveness, and its identity became more shaped by "the culture's story rather than by God's mission".[4] The problem for the church wasn't that it had become part of the establishment, nor that it found itself in the centre, but rather that it surrendered to the seductive temptations of these new social circumstances. The church was in the midst of what Oliver O'Donovan calls "a more hospitable cultural context, [and] Christians forgot their unique story and identity."[5]

The church enjoyed its status in the West until the Enlightenment. The Enlightenment "sought to establish reason over revelation through philosophy and science, eventually forcing a separation of the power of the church from that of the state."[6] The ensuing impact of human autonomy, individualism and reason had this earth-shattering impact upon Christianity in the public sphere. Though there were other contributing factors, with reason replacing faith as the controlling impulse, the church "lost its

1. Gibbs, *Rebirth of the Church*, 6.

2. Guder, *Continuing Conversion*, 85.

3. Gibbs, *Rebirth of the Church*, 7.

4. Goheen, *Light to the Nations*, 9.

5. O'Donovan, *Desire*, 212-13.

6. Hirsch, *Forgotten Ways*, 60.

position of privilege".[7] Instead of the church being at the centre of Western culture, the culture became secularized, which Hirsch describes as:

> that process whereby the church was taken from the centre of culture (as in the Christendom period) and increasingly pushed to the margins.[8]

And so, having lost the place they once enjoyed in the Christendom culture, Eddie Gibbs notes:

> Across the theological spectrum, local churches and denominations are struggling to redefine the church in response to the new challenges they are facing. The debate and experimentation are taking place across a range of traditions, from Anabaptist to Anglican, embracing both long-standing congregations and recent church plants.[9]

One of the reasons for this is an all-too heavy reliance on the 'Christendom' model of church. Churches that feel as though they've been left behind by the rapid cultural changes seen in the decline of Christendom aren't necessarily living up to their calling. The very characteristics of the concept of Christendom give us insight into why this might be the case.

Alan Hirsch in *The Forgotten Ways* outlines some important characteristics of Christendom[10]: It has an attractional mode of engagement rather than a sending or 'mission' mindset. This mode is fixated on the "good old days" of Christendom. There's a longing that harks back to a time where attendance was strong, Sunday schools (children's ministry) were bulging and more often than not, attractional modes of ministry and outreach worked. It also assumes a certain centrality of the church in relation to its surrounding culture. This is true of almost every church in every place. Our Anglican heritage which places a strong emphasis on the parish church stems historically from the church as the central place within the village. We will see how this can be of great advantage to churches but also contributes to some of the ongoing challenges for those in urban situations.

Christendom has had a focus on sacred buildings/places of worship which are static and institutional in form. As was mentioned in the introduction, in the case of my previous local context (and true in other local

---

7. Hirsch, *Forgotten Ways*, 80.

8. Hirsch, *Forgotten Ways*, 108.

9. Gibbs, *Rebirth of the Church*, 10.

10. Hirsch, *Forgotten Ways*, 65-71.

contexts), some churches have retained a focus on institutional build-ings. Whilst many of these are beautiful in their design and even iconic to their particular suburb in terms of history and architecture, there are the all-too familiar stories and associated dangers of such a strong focus on buildings resulting in congregations turning inward, focusing on the beauty of the structure and losing sight of the more important mission picture. Indeed, where the church may once have been culturally central, it is now on the fringes. This is certainly the case for many churches not just in Sydney but throughout Australia in our post-Christian context. Losing sight of the bigger outward picture has, in some cases, led to the edge being taken off their influence, where their effectiveness upon and even relevance to their surrounding communities has diminished, where Sunday is no longer a special day, where secular hedonism has taken hold, and where in some cases secularisation is firmly entrenched to the point where the words of T. S. Eliot ring true:

> But it seems that something has happened that has never hap-pened before: though we know not just when, or why or how, or where.

> Men have left GOD, not for other gods, they say, but for no god; and this has never happened before.[11]

In parts of Sydney, this is most definitely the case. But what can be observed is that some parts of the Sydney Metropolitan Area still have a remnant of a Judeo-Christian heritage. The Sutherland Shire and the Northern Beaches of Sydney are just two such areas (among a handful of others) where, from our interviews, rampant atheism isn't the issue (though secularisation has taken hold and there's a definite post-Chris-tian milieu). Rather, there's a nominalism coupled with an apathy and a secular hedonism that makes the church, and the message of the gospel it proclaims, seem rather irrelevant when compared with what's avail-able in the here and now. For secularism at its core seeks to undermine belief structures and look for meaning and hope in other more "tangible" structures and ideologies.

A contributing factor, from Lesslie Newbigin's perspective, is that the church ceased to understand itself as a missionary community in the histori-cal and societal context of Christendom. For in Christendom, the emphasis was on maintaining a supposedly 'Christian' status-quo as churches operated

---

11. Eliot, *Collected Poems*, 167.

mainly in institutional mode whereby the church was seen as guardian of the faithful—the congregation is an inward-looking gathering place for the faithful to be edified and sanctified rather than a staging post for witness and service to the world outside.[12] Further, Church history is not taught in terms of the missionary advance of the church and its encounter with non-Christian cultures.[13] Thus the structures we have inherited are neither relevant to the secular and differentiated life of the West nor true to the Biblical picture of the Church as a missionary community.[14]

In the context of all of society being considered Christian, the church became identified less with the congregation and more with the clergy and even, as was mentioned above, the building. This was reinforced as clergy grew in status, power and visibility to the end where it became apparent that "the church consisted of the clergy."[15] Thus, as Gibbs puts it: "Churches in the western world have been shaped by the Christendom paradigm in which they occupied a privileged position as a central pillar of society and guardian of its beliefs and values."[16]

Van Gelder and Zscheile conclude that "many denominations . . . still reflect the assumptions of industrial bureaucracies in their (1) centralisation of authority, communication and resources, (2) regulatory approach to controlling and managing ministry; and (3) rigidity."[17]

It ought to be of little surprise then, that in our current context, we acutely feel the collapse of Christendom. With the transition into this post-Christendom era, the church has gradually lost its prominent position in society. Over the years across the West, we've witnessed a gradual erosion. The growing influence of secularisation and pluralism in the 1960s saw cracks open within Christendom, that "eventually pushed the church to the margins and radically changed both the nature of Christian ministry within the church and the church's mission to the larger community."[18]

12. Newbigin, *Foolishness to the Greeks*, 102.

13. Newbigin, *Foolishness to the Greeks*, 102-104.

14. Newbigin, *Foolishness to the Greeks*, 107.

15. Drake, *Constantine and the Bishops*, 126.

16. Gibbs, *Rebirth of the Church*, 23.

17. Van Gelder and Zscheile, *Missional Church*, 159.

18. Gibbs, *Rebirth of the Church*, 25.

The fall of Christendom means that churches now find themselves in a situation where they must witness to a society that can no longer be regarded as Christian.[19] Hirsch has noted that the American situation:

> ...for so long a bastion of a distinct and vigorous form of cultural Christendom, is now experiencing a society that is increasingly moving away from that church's sphere of influence and becoming genuinely neo-pagan.[20]

The reality of the secular age in Australia is similar but broader. Generally, people take different viewpoints about the place of belief in secular society but are happy for the church to be at "arms-length". The trend at play, for those who do hold to a neo-pagan or secularist view, can be seen by taking a look at the professional suburbs of (for example) inner-city Melbourne and Sydney. The birth rate is in the negative. Yet the sociological reality is that the more religiously inclined people are, and the more serious they are about their faith, the more babies they have. So what's really interesting is that this highly individualised life script of secularism basically destroys itself in one generation. Therefore, there is an urgency to the task of reimagining the church in its post-Christian/Christendom context in Australian society. But it won't happen in our own strength. Throughout history, in those moments of great revival when people turned back to God, it was when people didn't try to do things in their own strength but in the strength of the Holy Spirit that God moved powerfully.

Melbourne pastor and author Mark Sayers notes that the general feeling in our post-Christendom context is that "We can achieve self-mastery while conquering our failings and sins, all without God."[21] This spiritual narcissism and the preoccupation of the self goes hand-in-hand with the rise in consumerism and a way of thinking amongst "Nones" in Australia who, content to concentrate only on their material lot, imagine that they fully deserve what they have, as though luck or circumstance or divine benevolence has little role to play.

I remember a conversation with a guy one Sunday afternoon at Cronulla Surf Life Saving Club. As we stood on the balcony of the club overlooking the vista of sand and surf with the rays of the sun dancing off the surface of the water, we were talking about life. He told me about all

---

19. Nikolajsen, "Missional Church," 367.

20. Hirsch, *Forgotten Ways*, 50.

21. Sayers, *Disappearing Church*, 62.

he had accomplished in life and how satisfying it was to have been able to send his kids to good schools, have a meaningful job and live in this part of the world. When I asked him who he was thankful to for all this, he turned to me and said, "Myself. I'm thankful to myself for all this." When I pushed him on this to steer his gaze towards someone else the conversation broke down. In his eyes, no god, had met his needs for satisfaction—it was all his making. It was an astounding response, but it highlighted the secular hedonism I've already referred to. Indeed, this may be the most deep-seated corollary of secularisation and a reason behind why many have walked away from organised institutional religion—"because it didn't meet my need". As such it could be leading to what Mark Sayers calls "the disappearing church" where:

> Part of the pain of our post-Christian culture is found in its habit of ignoring and marginalizing Christianity, seeing the whole endeavour as irrelevant.[22]

Sayers explores this notion of the 'disappearing church' through the lens of Gnosticism's influence. Gnosticism, as a religious and philosophical movement, was an early attempt to retain the fruits of Christianity and the solace of faith while maximizing the individual's authority.[23] It moved authority from the seat of God to the seat of the human soul. Gnosticism has been a powerful undercurrent in the West with its religion of self and identity, influencing believers without their realising that they operate under a different kind of code than the one they profess.[24] This, interestingly, squares with the research of Christian Smith, who found that "despite the religious or non-religious affiliation of their respondents, almost all held to a kind of loose, non-binding belief in a distant God."[25] In her research on why those who now identify as "spiritual but not religious" have abandoned institutional religion, Elizabeth Drescher found that: "The majority of Westerners hold to a belief in a pleasant afterlife and a benevolent Christian-esque God. However, the doctrines of divine judgment and hell are ditched as repugnantly retrograde."[26]

22. Sayers, *Disappearing Church*, 141.

23. Sayers, *Disappearing Church*, 59.

24. Sayers, *Disappearing Church*, 62-63.

25. Smith, *Soul Searching*, 162-63.

26. Drescher, *Choosing our Religion*, 23.

The "No-Religion" Shift

The recent seismic shift away from the Christianity that shaped modern Australia to a slew of worldviews has meant people felt compelled to tick the "No-Religion" box in the 2016 Australian census. The table below from The Australian Bureau of Statistics[27] shows that the growing percentage of Australia's population reporting no religion has increased.

No religion(a) by state and territory, 2016 and 2021

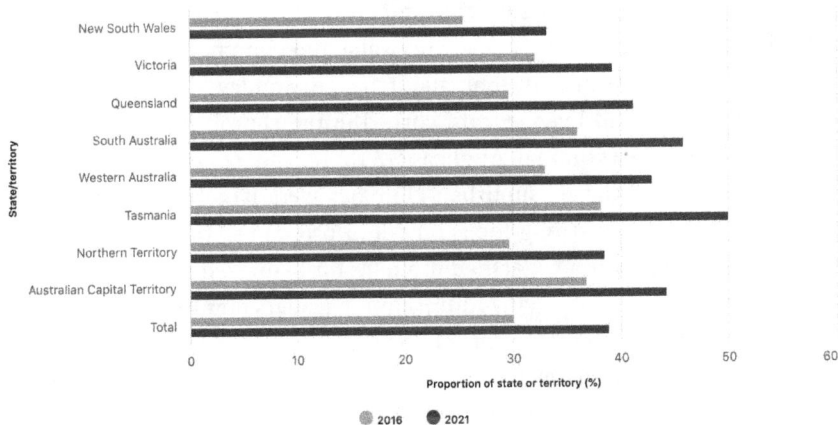

Source: Australian Bureau of Statistics, Religious affiliation in Australia 4/07/2022

Religion in Australia comparison.

Those reporting no religion increased noticeably from 19 percent in 2006 to 38.9 per cent in 2021. There was again significant change between 2016 (30.1 percent) and 2021, when an additional 2.8 million people reported having no religion.[28] Furthermore, since 1991 there has been a 22 percent drop in the number of people claiming to be Christian. The 2016 census showed for the first time, the number of "no religion" adherents (or at least those who can't see how religious they actually are), was greater than the percentage of Catholics: 29.6 percent to 22.6 percent.

While few people in any era—even devout Christians—have associated Australia's unique character with religion, it's fair to say that religious men and women have featured prominently in fields like history and

27. https://www.abs.gov.au/articles/religious-affiliation-australia.

28. https://www.abs.gov.au/ausstats/abs@.nsf/a59af5c52fdaoc7dca25704c001d21fa/7e65a144540551d7ca258148000e2b85!OpenDocument

creative arts.[29] In fact, it can be argued that Christians and Christianity shaped modern Australia.[30]

Nevertheless, Australia has been moving away from its Christian heritage for a number of decades now, to the point where we can be described as a post-Christian nation: a nation where the very memory of the gospel is becoming dim, if not non-existent. So how did this happen?

Although Australia has historically enjoyed a stable democracy, there have been some significant social changes over its time. The 1950s parish (a throwback to the English village model where the church was largely in the centre of the suburb) comprised many Australians who were God-fearing nominal Christians who walked to church. In this era there was no thought of growth, but maintenance. Sunday schools were for the suburb kids and Evangelicals worked in the church evangelising the church members (nominal Anglicans). Though there was a perception of declining attendance, suburban churches were largely well-attended, thanks, in part, to a strong focus on youth programs. The Billy Graham Crusade of 1959 was a watershed moment for Sydney. It left an indelible mark upon the city with many future church leaders pointing to that 1959 Crusade as the time of their conversion.[31]

Even with this energy brought by Graham's Crusade and fresh pushes for evangelism, there were signs that the plateau and indeed the decline of Protestant influence and therefore church attendance was about to descend into a new valley of secularism. The introduction of poker machines to clubs, Sunday sport, and a new economic prosperity along with the arrival of television in 1956, all combined to transform Australian life. These provided new distractions, and a materialistic culture of "selfishness" developed that was the antithesis of the Christian faith. Numbers, notably, at night services began to decline and, in some places, have never recovered. The 1950s generation who had been sent to Sunday school or youth groups by their parents, didn't necessarily adopt the same practice with their own children. And so the decline has only accelerated.[32]

More significantly, the impact of globalisation profoundly changed the working week, and with it, also weekends. The introduction of weekend trading in the late 1980s and early 1990s began to sort out the nominals from

29. Williams, *Post-God Nation?*, 169.

30. Williams, *Post-God Nation?*, 169.

31. Judd, *Sydney Anglicans*, 259.

32. Rayner, *Faith in the Fifties*, 2006.

the rest, becoming even in itself a significant cause of secularisation in Australia. Sunday trading altered the landscape further, since before this time, most people would attend church on a Sunday. It was really only the staunch unbelievers who would stay home to wash their cars or mow their lawns.

This resulted in a significant shift from community children to mainly 'church children' attending Sunday school. Indeed, the late 1970s into the late 1980s saw levels of attendance at Sunday schools and youth groups drop sharply across the country.

Efforts to curb this downfall have seen a rise in mid-week activities for community children and youth, but the translation across to Sundays has had mixed results.[33] Nowadays, our churches and Sunday schools compete with any number of more enjoyable forms of entertainment with little prospect of a return to the past. Indeed, it is now the case that only a small minority of children grow up in homes where religion is taken seriously. Thus, religious ignorance has become a major factor in the rise of secularisation. The rise in religious ignorance is also evident in the downfall of Special Religious Education (or Scripture) in schools. Australian author and social commentator Roy Williams suggests that some form of positive religious education is better than none at all, "because it means students may be nudged away from a position of near-total ignorance, and begin to think along non-materialist lines".[34] Even the move to push Scripture from government schools is a telling one, especially since even the government schools were originally set up by the churches. Even with these early church schools catering to the colony's children, it became apparent that government funding wasn't able to keep pace with population growth. Unable to supply enough schools to educate children even with their own financial support, the colonial governments soon would need to establish schools of their own. Therefore, a dual system was set up in 1848 with government support for denominational church schools. Standing alongside this was government funding of its own schools, at which the Christian religion would be taught on a non-denominational basis.[35] However, a number of states and territories have in recent times seen Scripture all but wiped from the government school timetable. NSW

---

33. One Anglican church surveyed found that after 10 years of well-established mid-week ministries including a playgroup and a Friday Kids' Club that not one family had transitioned to Sunday church attendance.

34. Williams, *Post-God Nation?*, 184.

35. Williams, *Post-God Nation?*, 184.

is one of two states where SRE still sits within the school timetabling framework, but even in these schools it is optional.

A larger contributing factor to the noticeable drop in religious affiliation has come through economic growth leading to unprecedented material affluence. The post-World War II generation known as the 'boomers' changed the shape of Australia such that the entire country, from around the 1970s, experienced a grouping of social consequences of economic growth: materialism, hedonism, and consumerism—the effects of which continue on today.

Any combination of these is potent and make functioning in community (let alone Christian community) difficult. Across our Australian society, there has been little or no increase in levels of national thankfulness, civility or generosity, and instead numerous unwelcome side effects: increased working hours, a plummeting birth rate and precipitously, a significant decline in churchgoing and religious belief. Interestingly also there has been a breakdown of voluntary communal relationships, leading to a decline in volunteerism amongst a number of social groups. Unions, Boy Scouts, Girl Guides, schools, some sporting clubs and even political parties in our current cultural climate scramble for volunteers. Sutherland has noted:

> Postmodernity delivered with one hand a celebration of diversity and, with the other, an anxiety over belonging and a quest for roots. The inescapable facts of globalisation pull in yet different directions. If the church is to thrive in such a milieu it will need to have its own sense of identity clear.[36]

It's worth noting, though, that some groups are on the increase, especially along Sydney's coastal fringe and (surprisingly) in more wealthy/well-off areas. One such example is the Surf Life Saving movement, generally, and Nippers, in particular. Established in the 1930s, Nippers (a program of training for young surf life savers from age 5 to 14) nearly died in the 1950s but was then revitalised in the late 1990s, tellingly not long after Sunday trading also took off.

These (and other characteristics of our current Australian society) show us why the church ought to be thinking of itself as being in exile: strangers in a strange land, and also why it is vital for the next stage of church growth that think and act differently than the Christendom mindset.

---

36. Sutherland, *Kingdom Made Visible*, 2.

This re-think is necessary, because the church cannot go back to a Christendom "innocence", just as the church should not attempt to establish a "new Christendom" through political means.

Churches, therefore, need to come to terms with new cultural premises. The reality cannot be avoided that Christians now make up a minority in our society—the census statistics strongly attest to that.

Churches need to ask questions of themselves and their surrounding contexts that probe more deeply, comprehensively and painfully than at any time in the past. Alan Hirsch in *The Forgotten Ways* (2006) raises some of these questions, such as: Will more of the same just do the trick? Can we simply rework the tried-and-true Christendom understanding of church that we so love and understand and just by some tweaks here and there come up with the silver bullet or winning formula?[37]

Clearly what worked in the past doesn't work now. We need a new set of tools or a new paradigm—a new vision of reality: "a fundamental change in our thoughts, perceptions and values, especially as they relate to our view of the church and mission."[38]

As Newbigin puts it:

> The question that has to be asked—and repeatedly asked—is whether the traditional forms of ministry which have been inherited from the 'Christendom' period are fully compatible with the faith that the church is called to be a missionary community.[39]

So also Stallard asserts that we must re-evaluate current ministries and ask hard questions about what needs to be abandoned and what needs to be started. Such visions are largely personal. Reliance upon the older institutions, however positive their contributions continue to be, may not be enough.[40]

While our history as a nation is relatively short, the impact of Christendom has profoundly shaped the mission and identity of the Australian church and continues to do so in our post-Christendom context. Furthermore, in our context, the shift to post-Christendom has meant a shift to post-Christian. While Stuart Murray contends (writing in an English context) that the former doesn't have to mean the latter since post-Christian

---

37. Hirsch, *Forgotten Ways*, 16.
38. Hirsch, *Forgotten Ways*, 16.
39. Newbigin, "Developments During 1962," 395.
40. Stallard, *Post-Christian Culture*, 67-68.

assumes Christendom was once Christian, it is difficult to avoid the fact that we are "in a society that has rejected institutional Christianity and is familiar enough with the Christian story not to want to hear it again."[41]

Given the context of Christendom and the way it shaped the church's identity and notion of mission, the shift away has led to a renewed understanding of the church as a missionary community.[42] In the Australian context, it is more of a forced realisation that if the church is to have any meaningful impact upon our society, there is a need for it to explore different ways of reaching out with the gospel. This can be achieved by way of contextualisation and a solid understanding of the different contexts in which churches operate. We will look at this in some detail in Chapter 5 and also in the final chapter in exploring some possible ways forward.

With the realisation of this distinctive stance, there ought to be a determination to share the gospel with others, and an energy for mission. Rather than pining for the past, we can be equipping our people to develop a courage to lean forward boldly into the future, learning to think and act as "cross-cultural missionaries" in our own society and using whatever opportunities come our way to tell and live out the Christian story in a society where it is now largely unknown.[43]

Therefore, in this post-Christian context, it is incumbent upon the church to explore ways of recovering what it has been called to be: agents of God's mission in seeing His life-giving word taking root in people's lives.

Because our understanding of the nature and purpose of the church comes from the narrative of salvation history, it is necessary to explore the theological realties of how God brings people into his kingdom. This is, of course, by his word taking root in people's lives. And this happens as God's people, the church, carry out God's mission.

To that end, we now turn to consider the theological and biblical foundations that will help us think through our approach.

41. Murray, *Post-Christendom*, 13.

42. Nikolajsen, "Beyond Christendom," 367.

43. Murray, *Post-Christendom*, 13.

3

Foundations: Mission, Exile & the Church

The Mission of God and God's People

GOD IS ON A mission and the church is described as the end result of God's mission. Part of that mission is to carry forward the work that God is doing in the world, which began with the Great Commission in Matthew 28.

Because we are the "sent" people of God, the church is the instrument of God's mission in the world. As things stand, many people see it the other way around. They believe mission is an instrument of the church; a means by which the church grows. Although we frequently say, "the church has a mission," perhaps a better way of articulating this is that mission goes beyond the church, concerning "the world also beyond the boundaries of the church."[1] In other words, God has a church for his mission in the world and his universal goal or mission will ultimately be accomplished by his word and for the glory of his name.[2]

"Mission" is a term that has gained much popularity through its rapid rise. Everyone in the last century, it seems, is jumping on the missional bandwagon to the point where it has lost its coherence: "When everything becomes missional, nothing is missional."[3]

1. Bosch, *Transforming Mission*, 505.
2. Wright, *Mission of God*, 64.
3. Gibbs, *Rebirth*, 24.

Many churches have "mission statements" or talk about the importance of mission, but where truly missional churches differ is in their posture toward the world. A missional community sees the mission as both its originating impulse and its organizing principle. A missional community is patterned after what God has done in Jesus Christ.

As we ponder this, it is important for us to consider whose mission it is anyway. The scope of the Bible is the story of how God has brought about salvation for the world through the person and work of Jesus Christ. Michael W. Goheen points us to the biblical narrative of God's work of redemption throughout history to define God's mission. "This is the mission of God: to restore the creation and the life of humanity from the ravages of sin."[4] This chapter will explain in brief the main points of God's redemptive plan. The biblical foundation of God's mission is necessary before we can identify the mission of the church. As Wright puts it, within the context of Revelation 4-7 it is God who has brought about salvation for the whole world since, "Mission belongs to our God."[5]

What, then, is the mission of God? The concept of the *missio Dei* has gone through many iterations in an attempt to understand the nature of mission as not primarily an activity of the church but an attribute of God.[6]

Barth understood mission as being derived from the nature of God and was therefore grounded in the Trinitarian understanding of God himself: the classic doctrine of God the Father who sends the Son, and the Father and Son sending the Holy Spirit within the context of salvation history, expressing the power of God over history. This was expanded to include another movement: Father, Son, and Holy Spirit sending the church into the world, and in this perspective, all human mission is seen as a participation in and extension of this divine sending.[7]

This was an important theological innovation since it placed our mission in the hands of the sending God, making it not primarily an activity of the church, but an attribute of God: the mission of the Son and the Spirit through the Father that includes the church.

Mission is therefore seen as a movement from God to the world, with the church seen as an instrument for that mission. To participate in

---

4. Goheen, *Light to the Nations*, 19.

5. Wright, *Mission of God*, 62.

6. Bosch, *Transforming Mission*, 400.

7. Wright, *Mission of God*, 63; cf. Bosch, *Transforming Mission*, 398.

mission is to participate in the movement of God's love toward people, since "God is a fountain of sending love."[8]

Over the years, though, in some circles the *missio Dei* concept became weakened. The scope shifted with the language becoming more about God's involvement in history and how the church participates in that. With a wider shift to more of a pneumatological emphasis instead of Christological during Vatican II, a wider understanding of the scope of the *missio Dei* developed. The danger in supporting that wider understanding meant that some saw the *missio Dei* being larger than the mission of the church, "even to the point of suggesting that it *excluded* the church's involvement.[9]

While shifts like this led to a misuse of the idea of mission, there is no doubt that the concept can be retained as articulating a major and vital biblical truth: that mission is primarily and ultimately the work of the Triune God, Creator, Redeemer and Sanctifier for the sake of the world. That is, there is mission because the God as revealed in the Scriptures is personal, relational, goal-oriented, a promise-keeper and, above all, the God who loves his people.

All these characteristics are reflected right from the outset at the creation of the world, where God in Trinity is involved in every aspect of creation, and where mankind is created to be in relationship with God. The narrative of Scripture continues as God (in the wake of the Fall in Genesis 3 and against the background of human sin and the judgment-grace cycle of Genesis 3-11) made the great foundational promise to Abraham in Genesis 12:1-3 showing himself to be covenantally and eternally committed to the mission of blessing the world through Abraham.[10]

This is God working out his purposes throughout salvation history to bring to himself a people of his very own. The narrative continues to be traced through God's redemptive purposes being worked out on the stage of human history for the glory of God's name.

Within this narrative, God called the nation of Israel into existence as a people with the mission given to them from God through Abraham and other agents for the sake of God's larger purposes of bringing blessing to the nations. It began with Israel and indeed Israel really is the subject and scope of this biblical journey. For it is in Israel's chequered history that we see unfolding, on the largest of scales, the themes of election, judgment,

8. Bosch, *Transforming Mission*, 400.

9. Bosch, *Transforming Mission*, 401.

10. Wright, *Mission of God*, 63.

redemption, ethics, and grace. This nation, chosen not for any reason of strength or size (Deut 7:7-8; 8:17), is the nation through which God chooses to make himself known for the purpose of bringing blessing to the world.

Exile in the Bible

The problem for Israel throughout her history was idolatry. Israel's apostasy from God and from her calling can be best summed up in the peoples' demand for a king to lead them "such as all the other nations have." (1 Sam 8:5-6) This was emblematic of their failure as God's chosen people to live out their "separateness" as a nation of priests. Following this, the ongoing cycle of sin, judgment and redemption finds its nexus with the Exile.

Israel's Exile was tragic. It was the culmination of a series of events from when David's kingdom was torn apart, as the land was invaded first in the north as Samaria was sacked by Assyria, and then in the south as Jerusalem was overrun by Babylon. For their idolatry and faithlessness, God's people were dragged away from their homeland. The scattering of the northern kingdom by the Assyrian Empire happened first, in 722 BC. The conquest of Jerusalem and the southern kingdom by Babylon took place over the span of ten years, 597-587 BC. Second Kings 25 describes the conquest:

> *In the fifth month, on the seventh day of the month –that was the nineteenth year of King Nebuchadnezzar, king of Babylon—Nebu-zaradan, the captain of the bodyguard, a servant of the king of Babylon, came to Jerusalem. And he burned the house of the Lord and the king's house and all the houses of Jerusalem; every great house he burned down. And all the army of the Chaldeans, who were with the captain of the guard, broke down the walls around Jerusalem. And the rest of the people who were left in the city and the deserters who had deserted to the king of Babylon, together with the rest of the multitude, Nebuzaradan the captain of the guard carried into exile (2 Kgs 25:8-11; cf. Psa 137).*

Israel couldn't speak or feel or think only in a human way about this situation—it had to be also theologically comprehended because Israel had abandoned the covenant of the Lord (Deut 29:25-28, cf. Lam 1:4-5).

So how was Israel to respond? The book of Lamentations shows us that the only right response to this situation was mourning and grief. And within this, God called his people to faith: to wait for him to act in the future (Hab 2:3-4). The righteous one by faith awaits and looks forward, standing firm.

As the end of their term of exile approached, Isaiah encouraged God's people to continue to look forward (Isa 43:5-6). And Daniel saw the importance of confession and repentance (Dan 9:7, 17-18).

Exile in the Bible isn't just an isolated individual event: there's a wider context and it's helpful for Christians to see that. It's about the clash of the Kingdom of God and the kingdoms of this world (so Daniel's apocalyptic visions). It's about a deep crisis in the kingdom, showing clearly God's people not in God's place and not under God's immediate rule.

That in and of itself raises existential questions: Where are we? (God's people who are not at home). Who is in charge? (The Kingdom of God or kingdoms of the world?). In recent times, Evangelicals have been forced to re-think their position in the landscape of society. The death of Christendom has reinforced for many the notion that we really are strangers in a strange land.

While the Bible doesn't detail the rise and fall of Christendom, Israel's situation might be able to help us to think theologically about where we stand. For it highlights the problem we face at all times, in that Exile points to sin, death, and judgment.

Genesis 3 describes the implication of the Fall as being an "exile", as humanity is driven from God's place (Gen 3:22-24). In a sense, we're all separated from God as we experience the ongoing effect of our Edenic rebellion, making it a huge deal for all humanity.

The Return from Exile

The prophet Ezekiel showed that the end of exile is all about resurrection (Ezek 37). Similarly, Daniel speaks of the end as leading to glorious resurrection (Dan 7:13-14; cf. Dan 12). This begs the question, why was there such a profound disappointment when the exiles came home (e.g., Nehemiah)? The short answer is that other kingdoms were in charge.

Throughout Israel's time in exile, the emergence of an exilic eschatology offered hope of forgiveness and restoration to God's people as they looked forward to a new age in a new creation (Isa 65:17-25). God's glory would be revealed to the nations through the ministry of God's servant as Israel finally fulfilled her purpose (Ezek 36:25-38; Joel 2:28-32). The Old Testament points forward to a new community empowered by God's

Spirit, to live out its distinctive identity as the renewed and restored people of God.

In the Gospels, Jesus gives shape to this as he teaches his disciples about what their relationship to the world looks like: how to live as part of the Kingdom that has drawn near. The values that form this new community, outlined by Jesus himself in the Sermon on the Mount, provide a vision for the new Israel shaped by the character of God. In taking the indicative form, the Beatitudes (Matt 5:1-11) set the tone for all that follows throughout the sermon, ethically and relationally. The sermon is all about how this new community formed by Jesus ought to live within the prevailing order: going beyond what was proscribed by the teaching tradition of the scribes and elders. This was for the express purpose that those around will "see your good deeds and praise your Father in heaven." (Matt 5:16) In other words, the community is to be salt and light.

The Sermon on the Mount presents a compelling and deeply challenging vision for the church as it seeks to faithfully embody the demands of Jesus. The values it embodies will not make sense to the world, leading to persecution and the temptation on the church's part to accommodate the surrounding culture, or even to seek to become "relevant" to it. Indeed, our post-Christian context makes it all the more important to live out that identity as the "blessed". It is therefore incumbent upon the church to understand the dual reality in which we live. In Christ, we are God's people in God's place under God's rule, but we are aliens in a world that does not recognize this. How then are we to live, and engage with the culture around us?

The answer according to the apostle Peter, drawing on the Old Testament prophet Jeremiah, is to embrace exile.

1 Peter: Embracing Exile

Confronted by both modern and postmodern stories, the church needs to take on the biblical story. As Richard Bauckham has written, "The church must be constantly retelling the story, never losing sight of the landmark events, never losing touch with the main lines of theological meaning in Scripture's own tellings and commentaries, always remaining open to the never exhausted potential of the texts in their resonances with contemporary life."[11] The story of Israel's exile and restoration—as re-told in

11. Bauckham, *Reading Scripture*, 7.

1 Peter—is one way of telling the biblical story that is especially helpful in our post-Christian setting. The first epistle of Peter was written to encourage Christians, scattered throughout Asia Minor, to persevere. It's a letter of encouragement to elect exiles urging them to stand firm in the face of persecution and opposition. With an emphasis on being sojourners and exiles, it answers the question of how exiles are to be faithful to their true home in a strange world (2:11). The scattered church of Peter's time finds itself in a position not unlike that of Daniel: a minority worshipper of God amidst a sea of paganism, in constant danger, but nevertheless a recipient of God's special grace and provision.

1 Peter draws on the exile and restoration storyline of the Old Testament, on traditions about Jesus, and on the (as yet to be completed) grand conclusion of the story. This is reflected as Peter calls a group of God's people to live in the first century as a chosen, scattered people. Peter writes, " . . . conduct yourselves with fear throughout the time of your exile" (1:17). In addressing the different recipients, he describes them as "elect exiles of the Dispersion."[12] (1:1) This terminology is then marked by such terms as *parepidhmos* (1:1; 2:11), *diaspora* (1:1), and *paroikos* (2:11). *Parepidhmos* is rare in the New Testament; Hebrews 11:13 gives it a metaphorical sense, referring to those whose real home is heaven but who are sojourners on earth. Helpfully, Edwards points out that Peter uses these terms as a rhetorical device to emphasize how his readers, like immigrants throughout time, are socially disconnected from the dominant culture.[13] Achtemeier also lends his voice to this when he writes that "the whole tenor of 1 Peter . . . argues for this [diaspora] to be metaphorical, and hence refer to all Christians."[14] This is helpful to our overall discussion, as the research shows that our churches too are socially disconnected from our culture, meaning that it's not a stretch for us to see ourselves as exiles today. For Peter writing to the aliens in Asia Minor, this affirms their status as the elect who are declared to be:

> . . . a chosen race, a royal priesthood, a holy nation, a people for his own possession, that you may proclaim the excellencies of him who called you out of darkness into his marvellous light. Once you were not a people, but now you are God's people; once you had not received mercy, but now you have received mercy. (2:9-10)

12. Quotations in this section are taken from the English Standard Version (ESV).

13. Edwards, *1 Peter*, 21.

14. Achtemeier, *1 Peter*, 82.

While it can be attractive to lean on the idea of diaspora as metaphor, as a Christian identity, *parepidemos* has a deeply symbolic or figurative meaning rooted in Scripture. Their status as elect exiles (1 Peter 1:1) anchors Peter's audience firmly in the foundation of Israel's history. The reference above to the identity and calling of Israel from Exodus 19 gives them both a strong sense of identity in unbroken connection to the distant past and especially the Israel of the book of Exodus with whom they are encouraged to identify.[15]

Both the metaphorical element to Peter's use of diaspora, and the symbolic meaning of *parepidhmos* signal that there is a connection between Israel's mission in the Old Testament and the mission of God's people in the 1st century as they seek to live as aliens and strangers in the world through their distinctive communal life. Joel Green notes helpfully that Peter's audience does not share with their forebears in Israel the experience of exile in having been forcibly removed from their homes. Likewise, there is no hint regarding Peter's audience that their status as exiles can be attributed to a lack of covenantal faithfulness.[16] Nevertheless, like he does in the opening of the letter, Peter closes in 5:12-14 by reinforcing this exile status. The word *syneklekte* echoes 1:1, and the reference to Babylon (5:13) suggests images of exile and dispersion. The entire letter then is framed by this concept that the believers are at the same time an alienated community but also God's chosen people. Thus, *parepidhmos* could at the same time be referring to the scattered Christians to whom Peter writes *and* the Christian church, which is composed of all nations and may be indicative of the temporary or transient nature of the Christian church on earth.[17] This is not alien to the New Testament church, and Hebrews 11:13 is a clear example of this.

Stephen Fagbemi appreciates the significance in addressing the readers of 1 Peter in this manner. He notes how it reflects on the theological and spiritual identity of the readers as aliens and exiles. He states also how it points and gives some shape to the likely experience and social situation of the readers.[18] This highlights, some of the confusion and controversy surrounding the circumstances as well as the identity of the readers of the epistle. However it is my contention, as I will show later, that it was employed to underline the ethical and missional implications of their identity.

---

15. Green, "Faithful Witness," 287.

16. Green, "Faithful Witness," 285.

17. Clement cited in Fagbemi, 2009.

18. Fagbemi, "Living for Christ," 3.

Throughout the epistle, as he seeks to encourage the Christians scattered throughout Asia Minor to persevere, Peter shows how the recipients' distinctive identity will be lived out in their difficult situation. He urges the elect exiles to stand firm in the face of persecution and opposition. With this strong emphasis on being sojourners and exiles, Peter answers the question of how exiles are to be faithful to their true home in a strange world (2:11). Indeed, since it has become clear to readers throughout the centuries that believers are alienated from the surrounding secular society, mainly because of their faith, Peter wants his readers, and us today, to read our contemporary lives from within the perspective of the scriptural story of God and the life of Jesus.[19]

Let's take a closer look at the Apostle's letter.

First Peter opens by giving expression to the dual reality that these scattered Christians are elect exiles: chosen according to God's foreknowledge, they are the subject of God's loving plans for the cosmos from before the beginning (1:1-2). Having been set apart by the Spirit for God's service, God the Father's plan and the Holy Spirit's power has brought them into obedience to the Son. Through Jesus' resurrection there is new creation, new birth, indeed life:

> Blessed be the God and Father of our Lord Jesus Christ! According to his great mercy, he has caused us to be born again to a living hope through the resurrection of Jesus Christ from the dead . . . (1:3)

Notice that Peter stresses that it is a "living hope"—an inheritance kept for the future, something we wait for:

> . . . an inheritance that is imperishable, undefiled, and unfading, kept in heaven for you, who by God's power are being guarded through faith for a salvation ready to be revealed in the last time. (1:4-5)

In the context of first Peter, the Jewish Christians of the diaspora were away from home, citizens of another place. They're called exiles (aliens, strangers) because they have a home where they don't live, and this resonates with us particularly in Australia in our current climate. So how did this happen? On one level, it is tempting to think we've become exiles because our culture has changed (which in many respects it has). However, when Peter wrote his letter, it wasn't that the culture had changed (1:18 cf. 4:3). Having been displaced from their geographical homes, they were also set at odds from their pagan neighbours because

19. Green, "Living as Exiles," 313.

of their newfound allegiance to Jesus Christ. It was the change in *them* which made them aliens and strangers.

Thus, it could be said that exile is a result of having been changed and given a new identity, a new hope and a new future.

For our purposes it is worth exploring in depth how the elect exiles are called to live, by examining the concepts of identity, ethics, suffering, and mission. We will deal with each of these, recognising of course that there is a fair degree of overlap throughout the letter.

The question of identity

In unpacking this question of identity, the apostle Peter makes it clear what life in exile looks like for the scattered Christians in Asia Minor who have been redeemed from the empty way of life in which they used to live (1:18). Peter calls them to praise God for their salvation in Christ even though they may have to suffer various trials (1:3ff). This is God's plan, predicted by the prophets (1:10-12). The new life means a new manner of life. The passage in 1:17-2:3 describes how, having been ransomed from their futile ancestral ways of life and the passions of ignorance, they are now re-born by the gospel and called to live holy lives. Having received new birth, they are called to grow up (1:23-2:3).

This change of identity and therefore citizenship happened through the mystery of the sovereignty of God and the free response of man. They are the "elect" (1:1) and the "chosen" (1:20). They are also those who have responded to God in faith. They believed the message of the gospel (1:21) and have "purified themselves by obeying the truth" (1:22). Peter then employs a cluster of images originally pertaining to the people of Israel, but which he applies to these believers in Jesus: having been sanctified (1:2) and set apart as God's people, Christians come to Jesus as living stones ready to be built into a spiritual temple; they will serve as priests offering spiritual sacrifices; they are now a "chosen race, a holy priesthood, a holy nation, a people for his own possession" (2:9-10). Green puts it this way:

> As exilic identity is a matter of disciplined life oriented toward survival as a distinct people, so in the present, they are to embody the call to Israel in Exodus and Exile to be holy. As a priestly people, a holy nation they would embrace the missional vocation

to be "holy"—that is "different" or "distinctive"—in the midst of the Gentiles (2:9-12).[20]

Like the scattered elect exiles, we are those who have been redeemed; built into God's spiritual house; a chosen people, a royal priesthood: we are God's special possession.

The issue of identity is important for a group that up until the last few years we hadn't given a lot of consideration to: the "spiritual but not religious" or the "Nones", as they've become known. I have already established the sharp and significant rise of those who no longer affiliate themselves with the mainstream church. Elizabeth Drescher makes the prescient point that with our world in the situation where forces outside the self are telling us who we should be coming into conflict with, "who we really are" has shaped popular notions of "identity".

Drescher talks about identity as "a much more complex entanglement of the social and the personal, of predispositions and choices, of relatively fixed characteristics and more dynamic features of the self".[21] She notes how in the last 20 or so years, scholars have tended to focus less on what identity *is*, and more on how individuals, and the groups of which they're a part, *use* identity to live what they come to think of as, more or less, "good" or "meaningful" lives.

This means that instead of identity being "a given" or "a choice", it has become a process that continues throughout a lifetime, sometimes changing a lot, sometimes changing not so much. According to Drescher, "this narrative understanding of identity has important implications for how we understand spiritual identity among Nones and Somes."[22] When it comes to identity, Nones have kept a particular narrative going—whether it's because organized religion has let them down or they see themselves as creators in the story of their own spiritual lives,[23] they are shaped by a variety of historical and contemporary forces alongside specific experiences.

Thus, pressing forward, as we seek to engage with "Nones" (the spiritual but not religious) and even "Somes" (those with "some" religious affiliation), it is even more important for Christians to know who they are and also *whose* they are. Daniel and his friends were pressed into the civil service of the Babylonian Empire. They were able to carry out their tasks in

20. Green, "Living as Exiles," 315-316.

21. Drescher, *Choosing Our Religion*, 37.

22. Drescher, *Choosing Our Religion*, 37.

23. Drescher, *Choosing Our Religion*, 54.

public life precisely *because* they remained rooted in a different story. Consequently, they remembered their identity, remembered which community they belonged to, and remembered which God they served.[24] Like them, and the exiles of 1 Peter, it's right that we don't feel at home here because the wider culture doesn't match that of the church. It's harder to talk about faith, guilt, religion, or even God and assume people understand what we're talking about. The plausibility structures are really no longer there.

This is where it is important to consider and perhaps even embrace concepts like "experience-near theologizing": that is, not only exegeting Scripture properly as we seek to engage with our culture, but also learning to exegete human realities—realities that missiologists are forced to think about simply because missionaries have struggled to articulate meaningfully the Christian faith in radically different human settings.[25]

Thus, in a culture where identity is now perhaps seen as holding a certain "fluidity", the designation of the recipients of Peter's letter as elect exiles holds significant import. Peter uses the term "elect" more than any other letter in the New Testament, reflecting their theological identity with implications for the physical and social life of the recipients.[26] As has already been established, 2:9-10 is the key passage consisting of a declaration of their status, distinguishing them from the disobedient unbelievers of 2:7-8. In doing so, Peter underscores their salvation, and the role that God has played in ransoming those who are now God's beloved children. This identity is transformative as Peter, alluding to Hosea 2, highlights the change of status from a people who had not received mercy to now having received mercy—and notably, it is also missional. Again, Peter utilizes the terms which God gave to Israel, terms which shaped her role in redemptive history. In doing so, as Michael Goheen points out, Peter tells the church that the same missional role belongs to them: the church takes up that vocation to be a holy people and a priestly kingdom in the midst of, and for the sake of, the nations.[27]

In using the Exodus passage and God's designation of Israel, Peter intends for this utilisation of Israel's identity onto the scattered Christians

---

24. Goheen, *Light to the Nations*, 65.

25. Priest, "Experience-near Theologizing," 194.

26. Fagbemi, "Living for Christ," 5.

27. Goheen, *Light to the Nations*, 160.

to have a missional thrust. That is, at least one reason that God's people are chosen and beloved is so that we can be a witness to the world.[28]

The privilege of being God's elect has, throughout salvation history, carried with it great responsibility and expectation, whether in exile or not. For Peter, this is articulated in 2:9b, with the God-ordained task of proclaiming "the excellencies of him who called you out of darkness into his marvellous light." Alongside their purpose comes the challenge which is then clarified in 2:11-12. In two significant verses, Peter refers to their identity as "strangers" in order to call for a corresponding present ethical lifestyle. If their identity as the elect is rooted and described in holiness, their identity as exiles or strangers is a call to practically demonstrate their holiness in daily living.[29] The elect identity calls for a new set of loyalty and ethics.

Identity therefore is rooted in theology and history. Its theology derives from the inherited title of Israel as God's elect. It is applied to and redefined to include the "new" people of God scattered all over Asia Minor. Fagbemi notes that such a redefinition of the title is made possible only through Jesus Christ's atoning work (1 Pet 1:1-5) and by faith in him and having been saved not through perishable things like silver or gold but by the living and enduring word of God (1 Pet 1:23-25). This links their salvation and election not to temporary things but to something with a permanent and an eternal value.[30] Furthermore, having anchored their identity as "living stones" with Jesus as the chief cornerstone, Peter (as he's done to some extent already) shows how these elect exiles ought to live within an unbelieving society and how they should live with each other.

The Importance of Ethics

The ethics that flow from their identity as God's chosen people brings into focus the notion of being an alternative society within the dominant culture of the day.[31] Peter writes to these resident aliens who were suffering ostracism because of their religious affiliation and identity. His concern is largely focused on how good works in the face of these challenges has

---

28. Edwards, *1 Peter*, 97.

29. Fabgemi, "Living for Christ," 7.

30. Fagbemi, "Living for Christ," 6.

31. Seland, "Resident Aliens," 568.

missional undertones insofar as their missional practice re-presents the gospel to those around them.[32]

Their way of life is coupled with characterisations such as "good" (*kalos*, 2:12; he uses the phrase "good works" six times). The use of the verb "to do good" and the ethical exhortations when it comes to these terms, shapes much of the book from the section beginning at 2:12 with the focus on issues such as submission to authorities (2:13-17), warnings to slaves (2:18), how wives can demonstrate the beauty of the gospel to their un-believing husbands (3:1-7), and encouragement in the face of ordeals and suffering (4:1-11). In each of these sections there's a correlation between responding to suffering and how ethical living can have a possible mis-sional effect. Torrey Seland suggests that 2:13-17 could be characterised as "apologetic-missional", that by their beautiful living exiles can "silence the ignorant talk of foolish men" thus fulfilling Peter's exhortation of 2:12, while 3:1-6 is probably more explicitly missional.[33]

Addressing these issues relates directly to their interaction with the often-hostile world in which they lived. Joel Green points out that,

> As exilic identity is a matter of disciplined life oriented toward sur-vival as a distinct people, so, in the present they are to embody the call to Israel in Exodus and Exile to be holy. As a priestly people, a holy nation, they are called to embrace the missional vocation to be "holy"—different or distinctive—in the midst of the Gentiles.[34]

In other words, it is clear from 1 Peter that their behaviour or Chris-tian ethic (i.e., holiness, or doing good) is firmly grounded in their identity. Of course, what also becomes clear throughout the letter is that this very behaviour is what leads to them being reviled "for the name of Christ".

The Paradox of Suffering

This leads us, then, to consider one of the great paradoxes contained in 1 Peter: the suggestion that the recipients are suffering because they no longer live according to their old manner of life (4:3-4). It appears it was their new religious identity with its moral implications that brought about

32. Seland, "Resident Aliens," 570.
33. Seland, "Resident Aliens," 570.
34. Green, "Living as Exiles," 315-16.

trials and difficulties, which eventually classified them among the socially alienated and oppressed in the society.[35]

Green notes that while it is important for the elect exiles to identify themselves with Israel in the reality of being the new people of God, there remains also the importance of grasping that being a part of the whole narrative is itself determined by Jesus and the journey of salvation and eschatological hope that accompanies this. He writes: "The Israel into whose history Peter writes is *Israel as interpreted* by the suffering, death, resurrection, ascension and pending revelation of Jesus Christ." (emphasis original)[36] This is helpful, because of the way Jesus' life (particularly his suffering) is time and again held up in the letter as an example to Christians of how to live well as aliens and exiles in the world. As Peter outlines what this looks like pertaining to character and behaviour, it is of particular interest to us that Peter's concern isn't to see Christian communities segregated from the wider world, rather it is to tie them firmly to their centre.[37] Green notes that Peter doesn't counsel retreat from the world (something already touched on) as though holiness leads to a stance of isolation. On the contrary, Peter's recipients are called to work out what holiness looks like in practice, in the imperative to keep their conduct honourable among the Gentiles, as those who have been called out of darkness into God's marvellous light (2:9). Underlying all this is the *means* by which these elect exiles have been called. For as those who have been born again to a 'living hope' and to an undefiled, imperishable and unfading inheritance through Jesus' resurrection from the dead (1:3-4), Peter's readers are able to rejoice in that truth and the protected salvation that goes with it (1:5), even though they may have suffered grief in various kinds of trials. Peter goes on to say that this salvation which God's people enjoy and look forward to is the salvation which the prophets of the Old Testament looked for but never found. The prophets talked about the things that would happen to Jesus: their message was the sufferings of Christ and the glories that would follow (1:10-12). And what is important to see here is that Jesus set the pattern: suffering followed by glory. The scattered exiles in Asia Minor experienced verbal slander and malicious accusations, hostility and marginalization, as Jesus did in being reviled (2:23). Indeed, he suffered the ultimate marginalization, when "he himself bore our sins in his body on the tree so that we might die to sin and live for righteousness. By his wounds

35. Fagbemi, "Living for Christ," 6.
36. Green, "Living as Exiles," 315.
37. Green, "Living as Exiles," 315.

you have been healed." (1:24) Jesus is held up again and again as the example of how to endure suffering: "To this you were called, because Christ suffered for you, leaving you an example, that you should follow in his steps." (2:21) Again in 4:1, "since Christ suffered in his body, arm yourselves with the same attitude."

The logic then of Peter's Christology is grounded in and oriented toward the new lives of those who are enabled and called to follow Christ.[38] This is encapsulated at the cross, which is the ultimate expression of marginalisation for followers of Jesus, who are called to take up their cross daily, experiencing that marginalisation and hostility.[39] It follows then that though the recipients "may have had to suffer grief in all kinds of trials" (1:6), their lives in the world are to be lived in such a way that those who speak against them and accuse them of doing wrong "may see your good deeds and glorify God on the day of visitation." (2:12) Indeed, in the section that follows from 2:13-3:18, a number of examples of Christian witness are given in different aspects of life for precisely the purpose of winning over those with whom they interact on a regular basis (e.g., 2:15; 3:1-2).

Peter tells the elect exiles and strangers that they ought to expect opposition which, alongside hostility and suffering, is a major theme in the letter. Peter writes: "do not be surprised at the fiery ordeal that has come upon you to test you, as though something strange is happening to you." (4:12) For Peter, opposition is the norm for followers of Jesus because they are exiles and strangers in the same way that Jesus himself was an exile and stranger. Indeed, this is where Jesus serves as the great example because while suffering and hostility can make evangelism uncomfortable, the task of Christians now, as it was then, is not to shrink back but to be bold. For even in the face of hostility God's people are still called to proclamation, recognising that like in Peter's time evangelism through gospel promotion of living beautiful lives can have a profound impact.

While personal hostility is not commonplace in Western Christian contexts, we still operate in a culture that is hostile to Christianity.[40] We

38. Green, "Faithful Witness," 289.

39. Timmis and Chester, *Everyday Church*, 35.

40. It's important to note that just because persecution or hostility doesn't look like it does in other countries like China or North Korea or Iraq, it doesn't mean in our Western contexts that we don't receive personal hostility. There have been numerous recent examples in churches over issues of human sexuality. For example, people in workplaces have been removed from their jobs or have even lost their livelihoods over support of the biblical Judeo-Christian traditional understanding of marriage.

need to remember that haters of the human race have been around for a long time. Even in the 1st century, Christians were inconvenient (2:15, 3:9, 14, 16; 4:4), meaning it's not unnatural therefore for Christians to face opposition, and indeed they ought to expect it. Four reasons might be given (and of course there would be others), for the hostility they face: (1) The recipients' union with Christ (4:13, 14, 16). (2) They're called to not join in the immoral behaviour of their unbelieving neighbours (4:4). (3) For doing good, or for no good reason (2:20; 3:14). (4) Because of immoral behaviour (4:15).

Peter does not commend those who suffer because of wrongs they themselves have done. His emphasis in the letter, rather, is on the first three. In fact, the first, as has already been intimated, sets the tone for the others. It's precisely because of their faith in Christ and their union with him that the recipients are foreign to those around them. As Karin Jobes suggests, "because all Christians are citizens of God's holy nation, they are to understand themselves as resident aliens and foreigners wherever they may be residing".[41] Thus in so doing, and alongside the call to abstain from fleshly desires, the exiles in Asia Minor were treated with suspicion: thought of as strange for not plunging into the same kind of practices when it came to ethics and morality as per the second point above. As such, they experienced a moral estrangement in society as a consequence of not sharing in society's values and customs.[42] Although Peter doesn't shed any specific light on what accusations of wrongdoing were levelled at Christians for what was regarded by some sections of society as reprehensible behaviour, we can ascertain from some 2nd century writings that there could have been charges such as "cannibalism, incest and atheism" thanks to a misunderstanding of the Christian practices of 'eating' Christ's body in the Lord's Supper, of marrying their Christian "brothers' and 'sisters", and of not having any images of their God in their worship.[43]

At any rate, how ought these believers respond to opposition? With what seems to be an important thrust of the letter, the imperative is to show honourable conduct among the Gentiles. While there's not a full list, it's not difficult to gather from the letter that 'good conduct' is included amongst qualities like compassion, self-discipline, humility, love, hospitality and the characteristic of godly submission.

41. Jobes, *1 Peter*, 169.

42. Jobes, *1 Peter*, 169.

43. Achtemeier, *1 Peter*, 177.

Furthermore, like Jesus, Peter calls the exiles to commit themselves to their faithful Creator (4:19), the one who is the judge of the living and the dead (4:6) and who will vindicate God's people at the proper time, just as he vindicated Christ by raising him from the dead. He is also the God who has given them a glorious inheritance (1:4-5) and an enduring and sure hope. He is the one who is able to make them strong, firm, and steadfast (5:10).

Having committed themselves to God, exiles and strangers find joy and honour in opposition. "Rejoice that you participate in the sufferings of Christ, so that you may be overjoyed when his glory is revealed"; "you are blessed, for the Spirit of glory . . . rests on you"; "praise God that you bear [the name of Christ]." (4:13-16) Rejoicing appropriately in the face of opposition is juxtaposed with the fear and fright which hostility naturally engenders (3:14).

Within this, the exile and stranger patiently endures and refuses to take revenge. "Do not repay evil with evil or insult with insult. On the contrary, repay evil with blessing" (3:9). When the Christian responds with hope instead of fear, and blessing instead of insult, the natural response of the persecutor will be surprise. When the questions are asked, Christians are called to always be ready with an answer and then to respond with gentleness and a clear conscience (3:15-16).

It follows then that Peter encourages his congregation to avoid any unnecessary conflict by always doing what is right, since it's of no benefit to suffer for doing wrong. Peter asserts that living well in the world brings glory to God (2:11-12). And though it may not deflect all hostility, Peter reminds the scattered exiles that whatever hostility or suffering they face, Christ faced it in his suffering (2:21). Indeed, there are brothers going through similar fiery trials (5:9). In the end, hostility towards Christians simply because of identification with Christ appears to be part of the normal Christian life in most places and ages.

This is the air we now breathe. A current and noteworthy example is seen surrounding the issue of same-sex marriage. It was first put on the table in Australia in 2016. It went before the Parliament with a decision made to carry out a postal survey in lieu of a referendum. With a two-thirds majority in favour, there has been a noticeable and palpable upswing in antagonism towards Christianity.

It's a significant shift in a worldview like this that shows Christianity is well and truly at the margins. Indeed, for all the talk of slippery slope arguments, when it came down to it, the same-sex marriage decision in

Australia was not a slippery slope. It was a precipice.[44] In his blog post, Stephen McAlpine suggested that with this decision, it makes the primary role of the church all the more important, as it seeks to equip the church to live in the light of the gospel in a dark world and to go out into the world and lean into it, in all sorts of brave and noble ways for Jesus.[45]

We shouldn't be surprised therefore: this is the experience of Christians from the beginning. If there was any time that we felt at home, perhaps that was the problem. Those to whom Peter writes who were once "at home" with their surrounding culture, are reminded that they have "spent enough time in the past doing what pagans choose to do." (4:3) Now, however, is the time for self-controlled lives lived "according to God in regard to the spirit" (4:6).

Peter points out that it is the gospel of Jesus, his death and resurrection, which sets apart the church as exiles in the world. They became a church in exile when they abandoned the false gods which they had previously worshipped and began to worship the true and living God through Jesus. They traded the perishable, dying, and empty for the imperishable, living, and enduring word of God (1:17-25). Note the similarities between this passage and Hebrews 11 which describes Abraham as looking forward to "the city with foundations, whose architect and builder is God." (Heb 11:10)

Furthermore, just as their identity is found in the God who called these elect exiles and raised Jesus from the dead, so also the scattered Christians' confidence in the return of Jesus Christ meant they had a great hope—a hope that is already living by virtue of the risen Lord Jesus. The believers' hope is anchored in the Parousia.

Having worked through Jesus to form a people who are his own special possession (1 Pet 2:9), God's people are to live with a hopeful expectation. Jesus' return, or the day of visitation, as Peter puts it in chapter 2, is the motivation for upright behaviour in the present (2:11-12 cf. 4:7ff). Having already come to know God's grace (1:10), hope is what sustains believers now while they await their inheritance. As well as having hope since they first came to be followers of Jesus, the living hope that comes through Jesus' resurrection is what keeps them going.

---

44. McAlpine, "Slippery Slope," lines 1-2.
45. McAlpine, "Slippery Slope," lines 75-76.

On Mission

The witness of the congregation in a trying situation of suffering can be, to a large extent, linked to mission.[46] Robinson described 1 Peter as a missionary document *par excellence* because it outlines the life and identity of the church—the people of God (2:4-10) seeking to live as a distinct community in the face of hostility. Peter's paradigm in the way that he interacts with the recipients, exiles like their Old Testament Jewish counterparts in Babylon, gives the imperatives as "exiles of the dispersion" (1:1) and "aliens and strangers" (2:11) a strong mission flavour. In calling his own city "Babylon" in solidarity with their exilic plight and in labelling them "sojourners and exiles", the instructions Peter gives the recipients at various points throughout the letter but particularly in 2:11-25, are not unlike Jeremiah's exhortation of chapter 29 to seek the welfare of the city of Babylon. His call for the exiles to be blameless in their behaviour: being good citizens (2:11-12), slaves (2:14-16) and wives (3:1-7), has a missional edge to it. Although their citizenship was not earthly, they were nonetheless to *engage* with the world around them.[47] Peter points out that it is precisely when this happens that living such lives among the pagans will in fact cause them "to glorify God on the day he visits" (2:12). Peter is quick to point out in the context of wives and slaves living out "the good", that they need not fear nor be frightened. Indeed, the very antidote to fear of those around them is setting apart Christ as Lord in their hearts which will in turn allow them to "always [be] prepared to give those around them a reason for the hope that they have" (3:15-16).

Instead of adopting a siege mentality as can be so often the temptation in the face of indifference or hostility, they ought to be "ready to minister to an often abusive world."[48] Thus Peter urges these "exiles" to stand firm in the true grace of God (5:12).

Goheen also understands the importance of the relationship between the church and the culture for missionary witness. He calls the church "an alternative community" which is formed by the reality of living the gospel:

> The members of the church of the first three centuries AD, living in the midst of the pagan and often hostile Roman empire,

46. Robinson, "Doctrine of the Church," 177. Cf 1:6-7; 2:18-25; 3:13-18; 4:1-6, 12-19; 5:8-10.

47. Boyley, "1 Peter—A Mission Document?," 76.

48. Kostenberger and O'Brien, *Salvation*, 239.

defined themselves as resident aliens (πάροικοι). The primary use of πάροικοι is that of a redemptive tension between the church and its cultural context. These early Christians understood themselves to be different from others in their culture, and lived together as an alternative community nourished by an alternative story—the story of the Bible—that was impressed on catechumens in the process of catechism. The entire catechetical process had this pastoral purpose: to empower a distinctive people shaped by the story of the Bible.[49]

We've already shown how God is a mission God and therefore it can be said that his universal Lordship is the "primary rationale and motivation for Christian mission".[50] In an important article, Mark Boyley, exploring the idea of 1 Peter as a mission document, outlines how God's universal Lordship is an important underlying belief structure of the entire letter. From the outset, 1 Peter sets, within the context of God's divine supremacy, a high view of Jesus Christ as the redeemer who is to be obeyed (1:2); the pre-existent one who will return (1:11, 13, 20); and the sin-bearing servant who brings us to God (2:21-25; 3:18). With this magnificent picture of Christ as the universal Lord, Boyley points out that Peter gives us, his readers, the theological motivation for mission and proclamation.[51]

Alongside this runs the idea of God's scattered people as being a blessing to those around them in the context of mission. Again, at the outset Peter is keen to remind the recipients of his letter of the great blessing they enjoy as those who have been born again and of the hope and future inheritance to which they can look forward. Together with that future hope lie the present blessings of sins forgiven (1:3-9; 5:4, 10), and life that can be enjoyed in a mutually loving community (1:13-22). More importantly however, to our argument about the imperative of mission, is the theme of living the good life of obedience and of being a blessing (2:14, 19-20; 3:9-12, 14; 4:14). The outworking of this is the imperative to show those around them what the good life looks like (i.e., what it is to be blessed and proclaiming this blessing). The way that God has worked across salvation history to bless his people becomes the key motivation for engagement in

49. Goheen, *Light to the Nations*, 7.

50. Wright, "Truth with a Mission," 11.

51. Boyley, "1 Peter—A Mission Document?," 77.

mission by his people. Thus, "the age of blessing to all peoples, and proclamation must be on the agenda."[52]

As we examine further the idea of mission with 1 Peter in conjunction with the themes already discussed, and how this helps particularly in thinking through what it means to be exiles, we keep coming back to proclamation. In 2:9, Peter calls for God's people to "proclaim the excellencies of him who called you out of darkness into his marvellous light". This is a high point of the letter. Having found refuge in Jesus the precious cornerstone, they have a new corporate status as those who make up the Christian community: living stones built on Jesus, constituting the temple and priesthood of Israel (2:5). Alongside that status is a purpose whereby they are "to offer spiritual sacrifices acceptable to God through Jesus Christ." (2:5) The metaphor of sacrifice offered to God as worship is also a pattern of social conduct which "dominates the central section of Peter in its entirety."[53] These find their expression in particular activities referenced in what follows—specifically proclaiming the praises of the God who has drawn them from darkness to light (2:9); conducting themselves in such a way that others glorify God (2:12, 4:16); and revering Christ as Lord (3:15). Each of these has a distinct mission flavour/focus. However, Peter's terminology in 2:9 is drawn from Exodus 19:4-6 and Isaiah 43:20-21, where "what was given to reassure Israel in exodus and exilic wilderness wanderings is now applied to these Christian 'exiles' among the Gentiles."[54]

Within the context of the restorative work of the Suffering Servant and his ministry to the nations such that they will praise YHWH (Isa 42:12), Isaiah 43 speaks of God doing a 'new thing' (43:19ff; cf. 42:9). He will gather the children of the Diaspora in a new exodus (vv. 5-6, 16-21) and this re-formed Israel will have a new purpose with an international scope: they will be witnesses to the gods of the nations (43:9-12). God is described as the one who gives "water in the wilderness, rivers in the desert to give drink to my chosen people, the people whom I formed for myself that they might declare my praise" (Isa 43:20-21). This is the picture Peter uses in the hope that they too might adopt Isaiah's purpose statement.

The ministry of the Servant finds its fulfilment in Jesus, the one who Peter will go on to say "bore our sins in his body on the tree, that we might die to sin and live for righteousness" (1 Pet 2:24). As recipients of this "new

52. Boyley, "1 Peter—A Mission Document?," 78.

53. Michaels, *1 Peter*, 101

54. Boyley, "1 Peter—A Mission Document?," 80.

thing" accomplished in the gospel, having had the example of those who preached the good news to them (1:12), and as witnesses before the nations around them of this new thing God has done in Jesus, they are to proclaim the mighty gospel works of their God, the unique and universal Lord of the world whose promised blessing of the gospel is for all.

Holiness or Living Beautifully

Within the framework of this mission proclamation is the significance placed on the recipients' lifestyle as they engage with those around them through different apologetic styles. Though some of this has been mentioned, it is worth highlighting a couple of aspects, for this lays the groundwork for some of our later suggestions as to ways forward.

In his book *The Best Kept Secret of Christian Mission*, John Dickson takes 1 Peter 3:15-16 and the idea of always being prepared to make a defence to anyone 'who asks you to give a reason for the hope that you have' and shows that it stems from a lifestyle driven by a counter-cultural hope. This hope comes from the fact that they were ransomed from an empty way of life and called by God from darkness to light—from an old way of living to a new life of holy living which in turn promotes belief in the Christ whom they proclaim.

We've already seen that this holy living, as well as being lived out amongst the community of believers (1:22; 2:1), is something directed towards a hostile world. The proclamation of God's excellencies must be supported by "excellent behaviour".[55] This behaviour is talked about largely within the domain of their social spheres of influence. Their behaviour among the Gentiles functions then as a strong ethical apologetic that will either help or hinder mission and proclamation. Unbelievers "see" (*epopteuw*) the behaviour of the Christians in their midst (2:12; 3:1-2). Because that has an impact on the eschatological "last day", when those who've seen their behaviour are drawn to repentance and faith (Boyley points out that 3:1-2 is clearly about conversion: the Greek *kerdhqhsovtai* refers to winning over), good behaviour is given an evangelistic potency.[56]

Therefore, Peter is at great pains to point out that no-one should suffer for having done evil themselves. Rather, as believers show what citizens' submission to authorities, slaves' submission to masters, and wives'

---

55. Kostenberger and O'Brien, *Salvation*, 239-40.

56. Boyley, "1 Peter—A Mission Document?," 85.

submission to non-Christian husbands looks like, this adorns the gospel and puts to silence any who might be tempted to slander them. It may actually win some over.

In all this, Jesus is the pattern as the submissive blameless one who did not revile but entrusted himself to him who judges justly, as believers are called to entrust their souls to a faithful Creator.

With a strong emphasis on holiness of life in mission and proclamation, the Apostle encourages his readers to take up informal verbal opportunities, and, alongside the evangelistic impact that good behaviour can have, be ready to speak out in a potentially hostile world. Indeed, rather than defensively withdrawing and bunkering down, 1 Peter shows us, as those who are also living as sojourners and exiles, that we are to participate and be a blessing to the different institutions and spheres of influence in our society, so that the gospel may be adorned and people might be won over, "glorifying God on the day he visits us" (2:12).

4

Thinking about The Church
and Its Mission

LIKE THE RECIPIENTS OF Peter's letter, we are exiles and aliens in a culture where we no longer feel at home. If we're to work through how the church is going to adapt to this particular landscape and engage well with our cities and contextualize the gospel in a post-Christian age, we need to understand what is the church and its mission.

What is the church?

If everything is church, then nothing is church. Due to the scope of this conversation surrounding the church and its mission, there is the tendency to ascribe too much to the church and there is the danger that we undersell it also.

A quick look at a couple of the main players in this conversation uncovers the following ideas:

Timmis and Chester argue that our love for one another is part of the evangelistic task.

Their focus is towards helping people think about church life together as being "on mission" in the ordinariness of everyday life, i.e., what it would look like to move beyond church as just a weekly service, to a community that shares life and mission. Can we be a people for whom church and mission are our identity rather than occasional events?[1] In other words, they see Christian community as an opportunity for an effective apologetic, and much of their work envisions "belonging before believing".

Mark Dever sees the church as being a vehicle for evangelistic programs that show God's love. He puts in this way:

> One of the main reasons that the local church is to be a community of love is so that others will know the God of love. God made people in his image to know him. The life of the local congregation makes the audible gospel visible. And we must all have a part in that evangelism.[2]

Dever further points out that we are all able to contribute to evangelism in being a part of building up the body of Christ.

The New Testament most often uses the secular word *ekklesia* to refer to church. In ordinary usage, this simply means "meeting" or "gathering". Further, *ekklesia* is normally used in the singular to refer to a church in a city, and in the plural for referring to churches in a region.

The New Testament understanding of church is relentlessly eschatological. In Ephesians, for example, *ekkliesia* is never used of the local church, but only of the heavenly one. This is also the case in many other places in the New Testament. Our true city and citizenship is in heaven, where Jesus is (Phil 3:20). Accordingly, in thinking about the earthly church, we must remember the 'now, not yet' structure of New Testament eschatology. As soon as we only emphasize one of these, we run into trouble.

It is no surprise to see that the main reason for this shape to New Testament ecclesiology is the person and work of Christ. "Church" is Christologically defined: Christ is a body. He incorporates us in and through his incarnation, life, death, resurrection, and heavenly rule. These three elements—gathering, eschatology, and the centrality of Christ as a constitutive element of what a true church is—find expression in the climax to the letter to the Hebrews (12:18-24 cf. Matt 18:18-20).

Furthermore, the theological foundation for understanding what is church involves Christology, pneumatology, and eschatology.

Christologically, the church is Christ's church (Matt 16:81-19), he is the Head of the Church and it is also his body.[3] God's purpose was always

---

1. Timmis and Chester, *Everyday Church*, 154.
2. Dever, *The Gospel*, 51.
3. Eph 1:10; 2:20-22; 4:16-17; Col 1:15-20; 1 Cor 12:12, 27.

to gather a people to himself. He did it in the Garden of Eden (Gen 1-3). He did it at Mt Sinai having rescued his people from slavery in Egypt (Deut 4:10), and of course he did it through Christ. This is because God's purpose has been, and continues to be, to bring people into an intimate mutual indwelling.

Just as the existence of believers is "now" but "not yet",[4] eschatologically, the same goes for the church. Thus, we read in Hebrews 12 that the church is already gathered in heaven now, while at the same time the people of God as the church are not yet there (Heb 10:24; 12:25-29; Eph 4:12-16).

It is on Christological and eschatological grounds that every earthly church is completely and truly church as they gather around Christ in the Spirit. Pneumatologically, Christ sent his Spirit for the formation of the church (Acts 2) and the building of the church.[5] Indeed, most of the New Testament passages that speak of church, speak in terms of "double edification". Christ is building his church in two directions: outward—by embracing people of every nation, tribe, and tongue, and upward—by fostering growth in Christian maturity (Eph 2:11-13; 4:12-16; cf. Rev 7). Ephesians 4:1-7 shows how the unity of the church flows directly from God's work in his Spirit as the Spirit works through the teaching and preaching of the living Word. We are united to Christ's body in the Spirit by faith and ruled by him by word and Spirit. This is manifested in the gifts he pours out by his Spirit. Faithfully congregating around Christ in the Spirit, and the edification through the ministry of the word in all its forms, are thus the two external marks of the theological and practical reality which constitutes a church.

In his thinking, D. Broughton Knox[6] insisted that each local congregation is the necessary physical manifestation of this fellowship which we share now with Christ in heaven. This fellowship, Knox wrote, "if it is to be expressed between ourselves while we still remain in the body in this physical world, must involve meeting".[7] The reality that we have been gathered by Christ, raised with him, seated with him in the heavenly places (Eph 2:6), that we "are come" (to use the KJV's words) "to the

---

4. Rom 8:18-39; Col 3:1; Eph 2:6.

5. Eph 4:1-2, 4:12-16; 1 Cor 12:12.

6. Along with former Archbishop of Sydney, Donald Robinson, D. B. Knox was especially influential in shaping our thinking of the theology of church in Sydney Evangelical circles.

7. Knox, "Fellowship," 20-21.

assembly of the firstborn who are enrolled in heaven" (Heb 12:23) must find expression in our lives on earth. This occurs as God draws people to himself, calling them into a relationship with Him. The first expression of this was as he gathered the redeemed people of Israel to himself on the edge of the Promised Land (Deut 4:10, 10:4). The purpose for which God gathered his people was so that, "I may let them hear my words, so that they may learn to fear me all the days that they live [in the land], and that they may teach their children so." The key element of the gathering at Horeb was the hearing of God's word. The writer to the Hebrews draws upon this language as he seeks to encourage people living in a world of opposition and persecution. As he strives to help them to see that part of this is the discipline of a Father who loves them, he says:

> See that you do not refuse him who is speaking. For if they did not escape when they refused him who warned them on earth, much less will we escape if we reject him who warns from heaven. (Heb 12:25)

Within the encouragement to not turn away, nor fall back, comes that passage on church where the writer refers to the amazing gathering of God with his people at Mt Sinai.

For both Knox and Donald Robinson, the church is the gathering of God's people. The language of gathering is specifically reserved for an activity of God's people which happens temporally but is also an eschatological reality. The ecclesiology of Robinson and Knox brings a sharper focus to what church is. The emphasis on the activity of gathering leads to questions of "what for?" Their answer was that the people of God gather for fellowship with God and with one another around the Word.

The determinative or definitive new covenant gathering is the heavenly one described in Hebrews 12 and also the one which John envisions in the book of Revelation. This heavenly assembly also consists of all those who are in union with Christ. And it's the gathering that Jesus has in mind when he famously declared in Matthew 16:18 that "I will build my *ekklesia*."

But this ought not limit the activity of the church to just God's people gathering around God present in his word. The presence of God is in the heavenly church which expresses itself in our local gatherings on earth and is an activity of the redeemed in times and seasons.

How then does this find expression both in and beyond the life and practice of church? In an interview in 2002, former Archbishop of Sydney,

Donald Robinson made the following comments in the context of ecumenical discussions of the 1950s and 60s:

> . . . you see they were transferring biblical assertions about the church "I will build my church" which were quite unjustified . . . In the New Testament you can see that the church at Corinth or the church somewhere else can be the place that God is using through which he speaks and says "Separate for me Barnabas and Saul." . . . The church itself is not the mission agent. The apostle is the mission agent.[8]

What then do we say about the task or the purpose of church? Or in other words, what is church for? Phillip Jensen has suggested that asking "what church is for" is perhaps misguided since the glorious gathering of Jesus is not an instrument to achieve something else; it is the goal or object of Jesus' work.[9] While we want to affirm this, it doesn't preclude the church from carrying out the task of moving towards mission as God's people gather around His Word.

The Church's Task

The Knox-Robinson ecclesiological model stressed the importance of the local church as an expression of the heavenly gathering, where God's people meet in the name of Christ and with the promise of his presence in their midst.[10] It is also a true reflection of the fellowship displayed in the Trinity: "the definitive mark being the possession that Christians share, the Holy Spirit, God himself."[11] Importantly, the presence of Christ in the gathering of God's people but also in the life of the believer is the presence of his Holy Spirit. In his work on Knox's ecclesiology, Chase Kuhn points out that "inherent within the body metaphor is an interaction amongst the parts of the body. The body metaphor highlights the *raison d'etre* of the church as fellowship."[12]

Robinson also saw great importance in the activity of God's people gathering together. This was so far the case that he viewed imagery like

---

8. Cameron, *Enigmatic Life*, 153.

9. Jensen, "What is Church For?," 20.

10. Robinson, "Doctrine of the Church," 110.

11. Knox, "Fellowship," 57.

12. Kuhn, "Ecclesiology," 162.

that of the Apostle Peter's "aliens and exiles" (1 Pet 2:11) as applying to the people of God in the world, but not the church per se. That is, the people of God are the broader activity of the redeemed, with church as a fundamental activity of these people.[13] Robinson puts it like this:

> The purpose of the ecclesia is that God's children, ordinarily scattered in the world, might strengthen one another's hands in the sharing of ministries to their mutual edification, and be renewed and inspired for godly living in their ordinary avocations.[14]

For Robinson, activities that occur outside of the gathering (e.g., evangelism) cannot be ascribed to the church. Certainly, evangelism happens in church as Jesus builds his gathered people through the speaking of his word in the power of his Spirit. However the Knox-Robinson ecclesiology shows us that as the apostolic gospel is preached through Christ's agents and as hearts of those who hear are changed—this is how the people of God are built up, encouraged and exhorted to abide in Christ, growing in godliness whilst enduring the difficulties of life in exile as God's scattered people. This means that evangelism takes place outside the church, borne by scattered individuals as they bear the gospel. By extension, it is by evangelism that the assembly of Christ in heaven and on earth is built.

Since God's purpose for his people is that we labour as his partners and fellow workers in building the gathering of Christ, the church itself doesn't have a mission as such. Rather it's the people of God, disciples of Jesus, who have the mission to build the church. Jensen argues that Jesus builds his church in and through the work of his people—"through our prayerful speaking of his word to each other and to those outside."[15] The aim therefore within the gathering is to build: through the fellowship of which Knox wrote, Christians are built up (encouraged) and even when an "outsider" gathers, they are built "in" as God's word is preached intelligibly.

How, then, does this ecclesiology help us? The answer is, while the church is not a direct agent in evangelism, as Christians gather around the Lord Jesus and as his word is proclaimed and they enjoy corporate fellowship by virtue of being the people of God, they are being fuelled for Christian living. Knox believed that at the conclusion of the gathering, Christians return to their lives in the world: and *this* is where mission and

---

13. Kuhn, "Ecclesiology," 81.
14. Robinson, "Doctrine of the Church," 109.
15. Jensen, "What is Church for?," 20.

evangelism take place. As Jim Crosweller puts it in his blog, "Evangelism is the instrument by which the church exists, but the church is not the only instrument of the evangel."[16]

Mission & Evangelism

As we think of how Christianity might grow, and even flourish in coastal contexts in Sydney, within the current climate the focus needs to be thought of more in terms of evangelism, and less of church. Crosweller describes it this way:

> My observation is that where church and evangelism are not understood in both close relationship and right distinction from each other we will want to always take the church out for a walk in the world when we should be taking the gospel. A church is a heavy thing to carry on your back when you need to move light and quick. Before you can step out the door you must launch a website, create a service roster, and when you do step out you need to keep the stepping out co-ordinated together because you are, after all, a crowd. Paul is often regarded as a model church-planter. But Paul painfully shucked off churches even though he loved them in order to go elsewhere with the evangel (Acts 20).[17]

Building God's church is the aim of evangelism but it is worth asking whether our focus on getting things so right with "church" has meant we've forgotten to think like Jesus, who, when asked (interestingly by the religious leaders of the day who were intent on maintaining the religious status quo) why he was always spending time with 'sinners' and tax collectors and worse, eating with them, proclaimed: "It is not the healthy who need a doctor but the sick; I have not come to call the righteous but sinners to repentance." (Luke 5:31; cf. 15:1-3)

This fits with the Bible's message centering around God the Saviour—the one who redeems, seeks and saves. There is only one mission: God's mission to come into the world because humanity finds itself in a hopeless situation, under the deserved wrath of God, and it is only he who can rescue us from sin. The scope of salvation history shows us God's mission to a lost world. This is accomplished as God sent his Son to us.

16. Crosweller, This is This, 2016.
17. Crosweller, This is This, 2016.

Jesus comes to gather his people, and to form disciples as a company of fellow-gatherers—those who would gather with him, seeking the poor and helpless (Matt 12:30; Luke 11:23).[18]

Mission therefore expresses the purpose for which Christ came into the world, and the purpose for which he sends us into the world.[19] Sharing Jesus' concern for mission which in turn will build his gathering, moves the scattered people of God to participate fully in God's redemptive activity in the world. Wright sums it up for us in this way:

> Fundamentally, our mission (if it is biblically informed and validated) means our committed participation as God's people, at God's invitation and command, in God's own mission within the history of God's world for the redemption of God's creation.[20]

Thus, our mission and call as Jesus' people is to be fellow workers with him in growing his church, by building people into his church, and this happens through mission and evangelism. Christ's commission to make disciples forms the climax of Matthew's Gospel. Indeed Bosch contends that the "Great Commission" at the end of the Gospel is to be understood as the key to Matthew's understanding of the mission and ministry of Jesus. He writes:

> It is inadmissible to lift these words out of Matthew's gospel, and as it were, allow them a life of their own, and understand them without any reference to the context in which they first appeared. Where this happens, the 'Great Commission' is easily degraded to a mere slogan, or used as a pretext for what we have in advance decided, perhaps unconsciously, it should mean. . . . One thing contemporary scholars are agreed upon, is that Matthew 28:18-20 has to be interpreted *against the background of Matthew's gospel as a whole* and unless we keep this in mind we shall fail to understand it.[21]

Bosch highlights the emphasis which Matthew places upon Jesus' activities among the Gentiles. From the role that Gentiles play right from the beginning of the Gospel (the magi, and the centurion of Capernaum to the not-so-obvious allusions to Gentiles and a future mission to them),

18. Clowney, *The Church*, 159.

19. Clowney, *The Church*, 161.

20. Wright, *Mission of God*, 23.

21. Bosch, *Transforming Mission*, 57.

the reference to Jesus saving his people from their sins in 1:21 points to the 'nation' who will take Israel's place as inheritors of God's reign.[22] From Jesus' spontaneous willingness to enter Gentile homes to interacting with 'sinners' and tax collectors; even through Jesus' Sermon on the Mount, Matthew conditions his reader towards a mission to the Gentiles.

Of note also is how Matthew never records Jesus actually taking the initiative and going out to Gentiles—they come to him, not he to them. While Bosch contends there is no evidence of a conscious Gentile missionary outreach in the Gospels, it is clear however that this changes once Jesus announces the Great Commission at the end of Matthew and clearly designates the apostles as his witnesses to the ends of the earth before he leaves them (Acts 1:8).[23]

Edmund Clowney stipulates that we mustn't isolate the Great Commission from the Great Constitution in the heart of the Gospel (Matt 16:17-19), where Jesus' response to Peter's commission shows what it means to make disciples.[24] In this famous statement, Jesus has in mind the new covenant gathering as described in Hebrews 12 and the vision of Revelation, the great heavenly assembly consisting of all those who are union with Christ. Jensen suggests that it is by the preaching of the apostolic gospel in the power of the Spirit that Jesus will gather his elect from the four winds and assemble them around his throne forever.[25] Thus in this way the constitution of the church has a missionary purpose.[26] So how might the Great Commission influence our thinking when it comes to our understanding of missional thinking? The key lies in what Jesus himself emphasizes in these important words.

The final part of the Great Commission is explicit with Jesus saying, "teaching them to observe all that I have commanded" (Matt 28:19). However, it's also what precedes this command that is worth noting. For the imperative in the Great Commission is not "go," but "make disciples". Bosch points out the concept of disciple is absolutely central to Matthew's Gospel. Jesus' words "baptizing them" appear to make disciple-making the focus of mission.

---

22. Bosch, *Transforming Mission*, 62.

23. Bosch, *Transforming Mission*, 50.

24. Clowney, *The Church*, 160.

25. Jensen, "What is Church for?," 20.

26. Clowney, "The Church," 161.

Payne and Marshall have made a similar argument in their extremely helpful book, *The Trellis and the Vine*. And while they (rightly) affirm that "we should be sending out missionaries to the ends of the earth and seeking to reach the whole world for Christ", they also raise the question: "But is that really what Matthew 28 is calling us to do?"[27] Part of their answer is:

> Traditionally . . . this has been read as a missionary mandate, a charter for sending out gospel workers to the world . . . But the emphasis is not on "going". In fact the participle is probably better translated 'when you go' or 'as you go'. The commission is not fundamentally about mission out there somewhere else in another country. *It's a commission that makes disciple-making the normal agenda and priority of every church and every Christian disciple.*" (emphasis added).[28]

Payne and Marshall's side point surrounding the possible translation of *poreuthentes* in the above quote does lead to some interesting grammatical discussion. It doesn't fit the scope of our research to go into depth about the structure of the text at this point.[29] Suffice to say while *poreuthentes* is a participle with an imperatival force, it doesn't make the participle the main point. The main verb in these verses is "make disciples" but the presence of the participle where it stands paves the way for the main verb to be fulfilled. As Leon Morris states: "Jesus was commanding his followers to go as well as to make disciples, though the emphasis falls on making disciples."[30]

Thus, the command is to make disciples of all peoples which is done by going and teaching people to obey what Jesus has commanded. It is worth pointing out that this by no means detracts from the impetus and the force every Christian should feel in the gospel going to the nations, and by extension the church supporting the sending of missionaries out to the field. However, for the purpose of our research, the focus on making disciples by going and teaching has important implications for how church members in coastal contexts ought to be thinking missionally and indeed strategically. In this regard, disciple-making is an important strategic gospel priority.

---

27. Payne and Marshall, "Trellis and the Vine," 11.

28. Payne and Marshall, "Trellis and the Vine," 13.

29. For a fuller treatment see Akin, Daniel L., Robinson, Georg G., Merkle, Benjamin L. 2020. *40 Questions about the Great Commission.* Grand Rapids, MI: Kregel.

30. Morris, *Matthew,* 756.

The "therefore" of 28:19 links Jesus' authority with the challenge to "make disciples". That is, Jesus' Lordship, by virtue of his resurrection, shapes our mission.

In the Sydney context, the focus on creating a culture of disciple-making disciples was brought to the fore in 2009 by the publication of *The Trellis and the Vine*. At its heart, this book proposed a ministry mindset change, designed to move churches from being overly focused on "trellis work": that is, programs, events and clergy-reliance, to a culture of seeing people mobilized for ministry through training and discipleship. I will make further comments on this in the final chapter.

The natural flow-on from making disciples is that followers of Jesus will then be baptized and taught (βαρτίζοντες and διδάσκοντες are grammatically subordinated). The force here is to make Jesus' disciples responsible for making disciples of others, a task characterized by baptism and teaching. We will focus only on teaching for our purposes here.

Throughout his Gospel, Matthew emphasized Jesus as a teacher (4:23; 5:2; 7:29; 9:35; 11:1; 13:34; 21:23; 26:55). Jesus teaches through sermons (Matt 5-7; 10; 13; 18) and through parables (23-25). All of this informs his readers of what it means to carry out the Great Commission, for it is the disciples who are now called to carry out that very task as Jesus passes the baton to them.

Behind all of these examples, says Bosch, are important theological (missiological) implications, particularly since for Matthew, the idea of teaching is much more than just a transference of information to someone. Within Jesus' teaching lies a call to follow him, which is to submit to God's will. Discipleship is determined by the disciple's relation to Jesus himself,[31] yet this comes back to "the will of the Father". For example, towards the end of the Sermon on the Mount, in the context of a driving warning against being side-tracked from the true faith, including dangers that come from the outside (7:13–20), Jesus says to his disciples, "Not everyone who says to me 'Lord, Lord' shall enter the kingdom of heaven, but he who does the will of my Father." (Matt 7:21). This is important because as Bosch notes, the central part of the Sermon on the Mount is the Lord's Prayer in which lies the petition, "your will be done" (Matt 6:10). He notes that what precedes and what follows fleshes out the core ideas contained within, all of which come down to the golden rule of 'love of neighbour'. This is Jesus' desire for all those living as children of the Kingdom in this new era. It was his

31. Bosch, *Transforming Mission*, 68

purpose in being sent into the world and it shows what being a true disciple entails: love of God that flows into deeds.

As Clowney helpfully notes, just as Jesus' purpose is the Father's purpose, Christians therefore are called to mission not just as disciples but as children of the Father, eager to do his will. In the task of mission, Christians demonstrate through actions of love and grace both holding out the word of life and showing compassion through their identity as God's chosen people, holy and dearly loved. Thus, the church's identity derives from its being a part of God's mission in the world.

Michael Goheen in his helpful book *A Light to the Nations* assists us here as he grounds an understanding of church (ecclesiology) in God's mission and story. He writes:

> Ecclesiology is about understanding our identity, who we are, and why God has chosen us—whose we are. If we do not develop our self-understanding in terms of the role that we have been called to play in the biblical drama, we will find ourselves shaped by the idolatrous story of the dominant culture.[32]

This is a helpful approach because the church is meant to be a "distinctive kind of people, a countercultural . . . community among the nations." God's people are to face "backward to creation", "forward to the consummation," and "outward to the nations".[33]

The Church and the Kingdom of God

We've already established the missionary nature of Jesus' ministry, and as Goheen argues, the central feature of Jesus' kingdom mission is to gather a people.[34]

In the Synoptic Gospels, the Kingdom of God is inaugurated through Jesus' public ministry. In Luke, this is announced as Jesus reads from the scroll of Isaiah, proclaiming that God's promised reign would be established as good news is preached to the poor, as freedom comes to the prisoners, as the blind receive their sight and that the oppressed would be liberated. Isaiah 61 speaks of the year of the Lord's favour, which Jesus says is fulfilled in the hearing of those in the synagogue in Galilee (Luke

32. Goheen, *Light to the Nations*, 5.

33. Goheen, *Light to the Nations*, 25.

34. Goheen, *Light to the Nations*, 102.

4:21). These political tones are more subtle in Mark's Gospel as Jesus announces the Kingdom is at hand (Mark 1:15). The Kingdom of God here is understood as both future and already present. Indeed, at some points in Jesus' miraculous demonstrations, he tells those around him that the Kingdom of God is imminent.

Alongside these announcements, Jesus consistently teaches that the Kingdom of God is a gift that has been given (Luke 12:32); that is to be received and therefore something people can belong to (Mark 10:14; cf. Luke 18:16-17).[35] It's also a realm (Matt 5:19). However in its eschatological framework, it is also something that will be inherited. From this we are able to see how Jesus demonstrated by word and action the nature of the Kingdom. From his teaching using parables to performing various miracles and by radically reversing what greatness and power looked like, not only did Jesus show what life looks like in God's Kingdom, but he sought to redefine and challenge the long-held Kingdom expectations of the 1st century—from being a long sought after political regime to it being a gift and a realm where receiving and entering are actions that mark a turning from other hopes and loyalties; from sinful rejections of God's rule to a singular hope in the one true God who reigns, and a Kingdom already breaking into the world.[36]

In Jesus' acts of preaching the gospel of the Kingdom, forgiving sins, calling disciples to follow him, and sending out disciples to minister to others, he demonstrated overwhelmingly that the way of the Kingdom is the way of seeking love.[37] The Kingdom mission is to seek and save the lost. If that mission is lost, the central message of the gospel is lost. This is because evangelism is an *invitation* to believing in and following the ways of Jesus.[38] As we communicate to people the person and work of Jesus, we are telling them a better story. A good example of this is Jesus' encounter with the Samaritan woman at the well in John 4. David Gustafson notes that Jesus ignored social prejudices when he spoke to her because he saw her as a bearer of the image of God and yet a sinner who needed to be restored to become a new creation, that is, to enter into the Kingdom of God, to receive salvation.[39] Jesus is graciously relational: in love for her and to show

---

35. In the context of Luke 18 Jesus shows the difficulty for those who cannot make his Kingdom the priority to ever enter it.

36. Hunsberger, "Between Gospel and Culture", 97.

37. Clowney uses the example of the Prodigal Son in Luke 15 to show this.

38. Matt 11:28-30; Mark 1:15; Luke 9:57-62; 14:26-3

39. Gustafson, *Gospel Witness*, 32.

he has something far better to offer, Jesus guides the conversation from her physical need of water to himself as the one who provides living water. Even as she attempts to avoid the issue at hand (her life) with secondary issues of religious differences, Jesus steers her back to the subject at hand so as to draw her to him and to show her what true worship is. As a sinner and seeker, the Samaritan woman came to accept Jesus as the Messiah. Her encounter with him changed her life.[40]

As the evangelist *par excellence*, Jesus shows how we can point people to that better way. As we participate in God's mission (for he is the one who has brought us from the dominion of darkness *into* the Kingdom of his Son), we recognize the part we play as "The People of Mission" within the grand arena of the world and salvation history.[41] As those in Christ, we share the identity and responsibility of Israel who were chosen, redeemed and called to live distinctive lives in light of that covenant relationship. And since "the earth is the Lord's and everything in it" (Psa 24:1) it is the field of God's mission and by extension ours as well.

Therefore, we must never think of the church as being irrelevant to the mission of God or that the church extends God's reign. Darrell Guder postulates a way whereby he helpfully recaptures the biblical sense of the connection between the reign of God and the church's mission. He puts forward a fresh approach to us being able to think about the church's life missionally, insofar as the church represents the reign of God in the scope of salvation history.[42] Elsewhere we have said that the Kingdom (reign) of God is a gift we receive but it is also a realm. Our mission will not usher in God's reign: Jesus inaugurated it but he didn't bring it to its consummation. God's reign will come since it has *already come*. Therefore, the church would:

> witness that its members, like others, hunger for the hope that there is a God who reigns in love and intends the good of the whole earth. The community of the church would testify that they have heard the announcement that such a reign is . . . already breaking into the world. They would . . . invite others to join them as those who also have been extended God's welcome . . . Here lies a path for the renewal of the heart of the church and its evangelism.[43]

---

40. Gustafson, *Gospel Witness*, 35.

41. Wright, *Mission of God*, 393.

42. Guder, *Missional Church*, 93–98.

43. Guder, *Missional Church*, 97.

How the people of God go about this task among their neighbours near and far is the topic to which we turn now.

Models of Missional Thinking

Having lost its way in the time of Christendom and with a renewed focus on the *missio Dei*, the functional direction of the church changes from a gathering in, to a going out.[44] Gibbs, writing from the perspective of emerging churches, contends that this led to shifts in emphasis from attraction to equipping, dispersing and multiplying God's people. He argues that the church loses its missional agenda when it focuses on a "come and see" structure.

Incarnational

Into this sphere came incarnational theology which was borne out of a realisation that the way of doing church throughout modernity (as has been established) didn't fit within a post-modern context and thus ought to be "de-institutionalized".[45] Thus it was proposed that a focus on a person's existing networks had much value, by expanding opportunities for different ways of meeting and organizing and inviting people to stimulating events, amongst other approaches.

In the United States, one outworking of incarnation theology has been seen in the emergent church with the creation of churches designed to reach different sub-cultures.[46] The argument, put simply, is that Jesus became like us in the incarnation event to reach us, and so it is up to us in a post-Christendom era to enter into the culture in such a way as to identify with and reach those who wouldn't ordinarily identify with the institution of church. On the surface, there is much to like about this approach as it models a desire to reach out to people who are part of a culture for whom the central aspects of the gospel are quite foreign. The incarnation and life of Jesus is therefore a good model, particularly as readers explore his interactions at various points in the Synoptic Gospels.

44. Gibbs and Bolger, *Emerging Churches*, 50.

45. Hunsberger, "Between Gospel and Culture", 100.

46. For a fuller treatment of this thinking see Eddie Gibbs and Bolger, *Emerging Churches*.

Michael Frost has done a lot of work in this area. In his book *Exiles: Living Missionally in a Post-Christian culture*, Frost paints a picture of a life-affirming and Christ-centred faith for followers of Jesus who feel exiled from both secular Western culture and old-fashioned respectable and conservative church culture. Drawing on Brueggemann's (1997) identification of the parallels between the dislocation and irrelevance of contemporary Christianity and the experience of Jewish exiles in Babylon, Frost argues that since the age of Christendom has come to an end, and because the church finds itself in a generation where life and modes of thought are no longer the accepted norms for society, Christians therefore ought to live "missional" lives so as to proclaim the gospel of Christ.[47]

Frost argues that if we're to have any real impact on our surrounding culture, church members need to adopt a missional/incarnational mindset. By "missional", he talks about the notion of believers living in close community with one another and through this community, being salt and light. Frost picks up on an idea known as "Third Places", originally developed by Ray Oldenburg.[48] Oldenburg said that Third Places were environments where people met to develop friendships, discuss issues and encourage sociability.[49] They have almost always been an important way in which a community develops and retains cohesion and a sense of identity. Taking his cue from Oldenburg, Frost argues:

> Third places are the most significant places for Christian mission to occur because in third places people are more relaxed, less guarded, more open to meaningful conversation and interaction.[50]

The logical extension for Frost is that in today's post-Christian society, any attempt to model your life on the life of Christ must include a genuine attempt to spend time regularly in Third Places.[51]

---

47. Frost, *Exiles*, 146.

48. Oldenburg, *Great Good Place*, 15.

49. Urban sociologist Ray Oldenburg defined a *third place* as a place to escape to other than home or work where people can regularly visit and commune. In his treatise, third places had a number of characteristics some of which even churches could share such as: neutral ground, a leveler, where conversation is the main activity, accessible, a playful mood and a home away from home. He argued that third places are important for civil society, democracy, civic engagement, and establishing feelings of belonging.

50. Frost, *Exiles*, 57.

51. Frost, *Exiles*, 58.

There is much to like about Frost's model: he has rightly understood the cultural landscape in which Christians find themselves. Furthermore, he is right to point out that the institutional ways of thinking, harking back to Christendom days, means churches aren't necessarily as effective as they might be in connecting with their communities.

His utilisation of Oldenburg's concept of "Third Places" as a new expression for the way Christians can be missional outside of the church certainly pushes us in our thinking of the place of the church in a post-Christian world. However, there are weaknesses particularly in where it lies with what we have outlined above *vis-à-vis* the theology of church.

As we've pointed out, the mistake made by some churches is to want it to play it safe, especially when in the current landscape we feel as though we are under threat. In one sense, the Incarnation is a helpful model to look to, especially (as we briefly touched upon) the picture painted of Jesus' mission throughout the Gospels is one of sharing his life with people, including the sinners. Frost argues that churches have unconsciously become the "Third Place" for many, and thus are sucking us away from the very people that Jesus would want us to spend time with.[52]

However, churches can still "follow Jesus into exile" and "develop closer proximity with our neighbourhoods" without abandoning our current institutions. We can still "name the name of Jesus in contexts where his name might never be heard", simply by showing people a better community and engaging in an authentic way such that we can still, to use Frost's words, offer this post-Christendom world the power of our trustworthiness, the quality of our relationships and the wonder of our generosity.[53] Living in exile without abandoning all that is good about our Anglican heritage means we can still pour time and energy into our churches becoming communities of authenticity. James Smith argues that in these attempts to distil and take church to other places like pubs, cafés or cinemas, we end up stripping away the weightiness that our worship carries theologically and historically. Further, as he puts it: "there is something good and beautiful about the ordinary grace-infused communal liturgy of the church that can point people to the Creator who is the only one by the work of His Spirit who re-orients and reorders our disordered loves."[54] Chapter 5 will explore

---

52. Frost, *Exiles*, 62.

53. Frost, *Exiles*, 99.

54. Smith, *You are What you Love*, 76.

this idea more as a pattern for a way forward in showing people the true beauty and liveability of the gospel.

For now, one of the aspects of "Third Places" worth exploring is the idea of community. That is, how it is developed and how cohesion and a sense of identity is retained through aspects such as promoting companionship and nourishing relationships by way of a diversity of human contact, thereby (according to Oldenburg) making them crucial to a community.[55]

D. B. Knox defined fellowship in a similar way, as "friends sharing a common activity or a common possession. It's not just friendship. It's friendship sharing something".[56] It is friends, he said, doing things together. And while friendship implies an idea of possessing one another, fellowship implies possessing something else in addition. Of course, fellowship can happen among anyone, but the mark of Christian fellowship as we've already outlined, is the sharing of Christ. It is as God's people gather around the Lord Jesus in the fellowship of the Spirit that the common possession they share is a person (Knox 1986, 77). According to Knox, going to church "is a microcosm of the fellowship Christians have with Christ and with one another, in the presence of Christ in heaven at the present moment, around God's throne."[57]

The Atonement as Central (and a better model)

With this in mind, we want to suggest a better model to adopt here that still allows for the "Third Place" as a way of harnessing community as part of what Christians do when they gather as church (for reasons that will become clear in our conclusion).

To do this, we need to explore briefly by way of interacting with two authors, what can be called the 'atonement model' of ministry and mission.

Since the central feature of Jesus' Kingdom mission is to gather a people, we need to consider the place of the redeemed community within salvation history. It is right to say that the narrative context found in the redemptive history of the biblical story and the literary structure of the Gospels, offer the original context for the crucifixion. Both are significant

---

55. Frost, *Exiles*, 59.

56. Knox, *Fellowship*, 58.

57. Knox, *Fellowship*, 79.

and, as Goheen suggests, connect the atonement with the formation of a "transformed community".[58]

At the cross, God's wrath and mercy come together. There, we see the problem, the penalty and the power of sin defeated as Jesus bears the burden of the sins of the world upon himself. In that seeming moment of weakness, the victory over sin and death is won. At the heart of the atonement is not only a victory for humanity, but there is a cosmic victory as well, as he accomplishes the salvation of the world. Newbigin highlights the significance of the atonement in this way:

> Down the centuries, from the first witness until today, the church has sought and used innumerable symbols to express the inexpressible mystery of the event that is the center, the crisis of all cosmic history, the hinge upon which all happenings turn. Christ the sacrifice offered for our sin, Christ the substitute standing in our place, Christ the ransom paid for our redemption, Christ the conqueror casting out the prince of the world . . . [59]

All of these images, though vast, when brought together, point to the new humanity the redeemed community arising from the Cross event. As well as being cosmic, the atonement also creates community that shares in the creation-wide victory over the guilt and power of sin (Goheen, 109). Paul describes it this way in Ephesians 2 with the result being:

> . . . members of God's household, built on the foundation of the apostles and prophets, with Christ Jesus himself as the cornerstone. In him the whole building is joined together and rises to become a holy temple in the Lord. And in him you too are being built together to become a dwelling in which God lives by his Spirit. (Eph 2:19-22)

Sydney Anglican Pastor Stuart Crawshaw who has worked in ministry for around 20 years has given much thought to this model. One of the problems as he sees it with the incarnational model is that it fails to take into account the far-reaching implications of the cross event. He points to Romans 12, where Paul, having spent the first 11 chapters unpacking what the gospel is, then moves to show the implications of the gospel for the Christian life. He begins verse 1 by saying:

58. Goheen, *Light to the Nations*, 102-05.
59. Newbigin, *Open Secret*, 49-50.

Therefore, I urge you, brothers, in view of God's mercy, to offer your bodies as living sacrifices.

And then, immediately following that, Paul outlines what this looks like practically for God's people when he says in verse 2, "Do not conform to the pattern of this world, but be transformed by the renewing of your mind" (Rom 12:2).

This is where Crawshaw perceives a problem for those who espouse the incarnational model, because in seeking to affirm a culture by dressing like them and talking like them, it begs the question: at what point do we actually start to speak into that culture and challenge some of the inconsistencies? As one pastor put it in our research:

> . . . how much can the gospel reach into a certain space before the gospel actually has to push against something. At some point you've got to pop the polite bubble and some point you've got to go, 'we can go so far culturally, but at certain points, the gospel should change you and the gospel should mean you don't keep going down a certain path.'

It is our contention that one of the difficulties with the incarnational model is that, in some cases, in an attempt to identify with the culture one can almost become too enmeshed. Indeed as Peter Adam puts it:

> The primary significance of the incarnation was that Christ was incarnate in the human race, rather than in particular social and cultural circumstances, however, as a secondary implication, the point has some power. Though we should remember that those 'particular social and cultural circumstances' were not without specific and unique theological significance, namely, the existence of God's people, a chosen race, a priestly kingdom and a holy nation. So there is not an exact parallel between Christ's relationship with Israel, and our relationship with any social group.[60]

This is where relational, gospel-driven ministry that's missionally-focused, must point people to the transformation that comes because of the death *and* resurrection of Jesus. That is, one cannot merely focus on the incarnation without considering its trajectory within salvation history. Jesus is both atonement and example, and the Scriptures make it clear that we can't have one without the other. As we established in our survey of 1 Peter,

---

60. Adam, "Incarnational Theology", 15.

> For it is to this that you have been called, because Christ also suf-
> fered for you, leaving you an example, so that you should follow
> in his steps...He himself bore our sins in his body on the cross, so
> that, free from sins, we might live for righteousness; by his wounds
> you have been healed (1 Pet 2:21, 24).

Further we cannot ignore Jesus' resurrection, for that gives shape to everything in terms of dying to sin and living the new righteous life in Christ.

For Crawshaw, since the basis of the atonement is the love God has for the world, the flow-on from this is for us to love our neighbour. He says:

> . . . with the atonement, what I thought is rather than being cultur-
> ally relevant first, what if we were—like you said earlier, what if
> we were loving first? So I thought about it and I thought well, the
> way to express our worship is through being a living sacrifice. So
> in view of Jesus laying his life down for us, we lay our life down
> for other people. And when Paul talks about being all things to all
> men in Corinthians, I think he's talking about, not be a surfer to
> the surfers; I think he's been willing to associate with people who
> are different to yourself, that's how I read that. So I think the first
> step is to say how do we love people who are in the surf culture,
> rather than having to be relevant to them again? And that's the
> starting point the atonement gives me.[61]

To summarize therefore, incarnational theologians take "Third Place" theory and seek to create a "Third Place" community in between the world and the church. For Crawshaw, the atonement provides a framework for actually attaching this "Third Place" community to the church. So rather than trying to create a culturally relevant "Third Place", the aim is to create a "Christian Third Place"; that is, you work hard on the community aspect in your church with the atonement as the framework and foundation. This is especially pertinent to our topic, as our research showed that one of the deep yearnings people have is for connection and community. Further-more, when one considers the communities of sporting clubs in general and surf lifesaving clubs in particular, there is something about those communities that draws people to them. We've already established that in a post-Christendom context, the attractional method doesn't always work. There is however something attractive about Christians showing how the gospel has transformed them, particularly when God's people

---

61. Crawshaw, Recorded Interview, 2020.

demonstrate the "one another" passages of Scripture in loving one another and carrying each other's burdens. Crawshaw proposes that as God's people do that, they show that with one eye towards their community they can invite non-Christians to come and see how they live.

The atonement model allows us to reconnect ecclesiology and missiology. It shows what a solid missional ecclesiology looks like; not something that becomes a survival strategy for retreating, inward-looking churches; not attractional, but outward focused, culturally engaging, meeting people where they're at, and showing them how the death and resurrection of Jesus changes everything, as churches bear witness to God's mission to see people rescued from the dominion of darkness and brought into the Kingdom of Jesus (Col 1:12-13).

When the task of mission is understood as embodying this new order, then every aspect of church life becomes missional.

Mission is about God's people authentically expressing their identity in a communal manner even in an age where it is on the fringes. Mission can't just be part of the church program: the scattered people of God must be missional. As God's people are "on mission", whether that be promoting or proclaiming the evangel (gospel), that is one way of displaying how God has worked throughout salvation history to bring to himself a people of his own.

We have seen that, due to the nature of secularism and atheism, and the rise in the non-religious, there is great potential of being a marginalized church in this world. At this point in history, the church is certainly the "underdog", and so instead of mourning our marginal position, we ought to embrace our cultural exile, recognising within it there are advantages to be discovered.[62]

Sayers suggests that our increasing strangeness to Western culture could be to our advantage. A solid theological understanding of our current circumstances as exiles in this world alongside a fresh vision of the centrality of the atonement gives shape to how we operate as the church. All of this, against the backdrop of the grand theme of Scripture, will give the church the scope to think better about how we engage with our world as strangers in a post-Christian context.

---

62. Sayers, *Disappearing Church*, 139

5

Sociological And Cultural Challenges

CHAPTER 3 ESTABLISHED WHERE we find ourselves in this post-Christian age by way of a biblical theology of exile. Further, having outlined a theology of church and mission, and how an atonement model of ministry fits with that ecclesiological and missiological basis, we turn our focus to the sociological and cultural challenges in order to gain further understanding of how best to engage with a suburban coastal context in 21st century post-Christian Sydney.

You can see across the cultural landscape of Sydney that some parts of the Metropolitan Area still have a remnant of a Judeo-Christian heritage. The Sutherland Shire and the Northern Beaches are just two such areas where rampant atheism isn't the issue. Rather, there's a nominalism coupled with an apathy and a secular hedonism that makes the church and the message of the gospel it proclaims seem rather irrelevant when compared with what's available in the here and now.

The ethnographic component to the research combined with analysis of the suburb of Cronulla and my day-to-day experiences of ministry in the suburb, allowed me to draw some tentative conclusions about mission in beachside churches with a strong surf club culture. It became apparent that I needed to test these conclusions by studying other beachside suburbs. These suburbs were chosen on the basis of their proximity to the beach and local Surf Life Saving Clubs. Through surveys and conversations with the ministers and also drawing on the experience of some Cronulla "community gatekeepers", I concluded that their experience is similar to that of other suburban coastal contexts and so the hypotheses of Cronulla appeared appropriate to similar beach-side cultures.

Cronulla: A brief case study

Consider the suburb of Cronulla within the Sutherland Shire. Nick Bryant, writing in 2012 for *The Monthly* said that the story of the Shire is really a study in geohistory:[1]

> Rivers, bays, the ocean and acres of thick bushland mark out the Sutherland Shire boundaries. Labelled by one of the most renowned Cronulla identities Joe Monro (1883-1966) as the jewel in the crown of the Sutherland Shire . . . [2]

This geographic isolation and the natural beauty that comes with it help make sense both of its favoured moniker, "God's Country", and its derisive nickname, "the insular peninsula". The names of its most famous suburbs also refer to the landscape. "Sylvania Waters" stems from its sylvan appearance. "Cronulla", or *kurranulla*, in the local Aboriginal language, means "place of pink shells".

Considered "the birthplace of modern Australia", it was on a rocky outcrop on the shores of what is now called the Kurnell Peninsula that James Cook and his crew first landed on 29 April 1770. Cook's portrait doubles as the council's logo. The Shire's flag also pays homage to Cook. It features the cross of St George, a laurel wreath and the globe, the ocean and two golden polar stars, which are taken from the coat of arms of the British explorer.

Though James Cook discovered Australia in the late 1700s, it really wasn't until the late 18th-early 19th century that people began to really take notice of this Shire area. The Shire was little known and rarely visited "out of sight, out of mind and neglected", according to historian Paul Ashton.[3]

Everything changed with the formation of the Holt-Sutherland Estate Land Company in 1881, courtesy of Thomas Holt who owned most

1. Bryant, "Shire versus Australia", line 128
2. Bryant, "Shire versus Australia", lines 1301-31
3. Bryant, "Shire versus Australia", lines 148-149.

of the land in the Sutherland Shire. As land was leased, farmers began settling in the district.[4]

With the construction of the Illawarra railway in 1884, the Sutherland village was put on the map, leading to its proclamation as a Shire in 1906. Even then, most Sydneysiders viewed it as a place of recreation rather than habitation.

Changes to land tenure facilitated permanent settlement of the district, and the sale of land on the Cronulla peninsula at three auctions in 1895, 1897 and 1900 saw a gradual increase of people taking up residence. However, it was the Holt Sutherland Estate Act, 1900, allowing estate tenants to freehold their land, which encouraged an increasing number of people to put down permanent roots in the district.

Pauline Curby notes that it was tourism which made the deserted beach first a village and later a suburb.[5] By the end of 1910 it had become a resort. And while the suburb had a 'resort-vibe' to it, local residents were campaigning for things like a local school to be opened—and so Cronulla Public School was opened in January 1910.

Such was the nature of the suburb that its growth tripled in its first ten years. The population boomed in the first two decades of the 1900s, and blocks began to be subdivided. "Continuous comment was made on Cronulla's remarkable development, more because of the rapidity of urban change rather than because it had become a place of urban sophistication."[6]

Post-World War I and into the years of the Depression, the suburb continued to grow; Cronulla Surf Life Saving Club was established by this time, and blocks in the northern part of the suburb were being subdivided and sold off.

With a population of just 1,960 in 1939, a significant shift also occurred in the late 1940s and into the 50s, where people who had been visiting the suburb for holidays and weekends became permanent residents. Some were retirees who converted their weekenders or demolished old cottages and built new homes.[7]

Only after World War II, with the availability of cheap land, did the suburb begin to grow. There were other contributing factors to significant growth in the population, such as the postwar baby boom, but also from

4. Curby, *History of Cronulla*, 2.
5. Curby, *History of Cronulla*, 22.
6. Curby, *History of Cronulla*, 33.
7. Curby, *History of Cronulla*, 88.

a movement of people from the inner suburbs to what was seen as more affordable housing further from the city.[8]

The low price of land was especially a draw for aspirational working-class Sydney residents, many of them tradesmen, who could not afford waterside homes in the eastern suburbs or on the northern beaches.

Between 1951 and 1961, the population more than doubled from 50,000 to 112,000. Almost 20% were from overseas, mainly immigrants from Britain, who were followed by the Dutch, the Germans, then the Italians. By the 1990s, little was left of Cronulla's identity as a holiday resort. It was then, and is still now in the 21st century, "a residential suburb that experiences mainly at weekends and holidays an influx of people on day visits".[9]

Ongoing development of the railway corridor and large unit blocks are changing the character of the suburb in what some have described as undesirable ways. Though it still retains a character of being home to a wide range of people on the social scale, it also has that feel of being a place where only the well-heeled can afford to buy. It is now a suburb of contrasts: deep poverty continues to sit beside showy affluence.

Culturally there is a blend of different pastimes and sub-cultures. Surfboard riding was introduced in 1915. By the 1960s it had become a widely practiced sport and pastime, but it contributed massively and was embedded within the culture of Cronulla in a huge way—attested to by the book-cum-movie, *Puberty Blues*.[10]

Interestingly, it isn't all holidays and surfing: the beach has become a place of memory. At the dedication service of the memorial to the seven women from the Sutherland Shire who lost their lives in the Bali terrorist attacks it was said: "The memories and bonds that were—they do live on forever." Official and unofficial memorials and ashes scattering ceremonies by the surf clubs in Bate Bay are commonplace. They celebrate the lives of

8. Curby, *History of Cronulla*, 83.

9. Curby, *History of Cronulla*, 109.

10. First published in 1979, the book *Puberty Blues* encapsulates the youth culture of 1970s Sydney. Written from the perspective of two thirteen-year-olds, it tells of their desires to make it into one of the surfie gangs that hang around Cronulla Beach. As they try to make it to the top of the social hierarchy, they learn about sex, drugs, boys, and ultimately, themselves. Over the years other productions have tried (largely unsuccessfully) to capture something of the culture of Cronulla and the Shire, including *Sylvania Waters*, *The Shire*: a 'reality'-based program that was largely panned by long-term local residents, and a movie version of *Puberty Blues*. These and other attempts at capturing something of the culture have been commented on elsewhere.

everyone, from the Bali victims to old club members. There is a special connection and affinity with the surf that is an integral part of the rich tapestry of the culture of not just Cronulla but other beachside contexts.

Though each ministry situation is unique and since this is the case for different suburban pockets of Sydney, it could be said (and we asked the question of those who live in the Shire) that in smaller, homogeneous and stable communities like the suburbs of the Shire or the peninsula of the Northern Beaches, civil society still prevails. Neighbours are mostly happy to accommodate one another and come to each other's assistance; the church (and particularly the *established* Anglican church) is still "respected" (i.e., participation in local cultural events, placement of chaplains in sporting clubs).

It is interesting to note that with the establishment of a new suburb within the Cronulla parish (Greenhills Beach), no significant community space was included in the planning. Contrast this with the expanding "greenfield" areas of Sydney where the Anglican Diocese has been able to secure land from the expansion for things like Anglican schools and retirement villages as well as of course, the local church.[11] On the one hand our culture sees the need for community and for churches to be an important part of the hub in new and burgeoning suburbs, but in other cases community space is swallowed up by trying to squeeze as many mansions as possible into a particular area. For Cronulla and the Shire in general, it is clear that one of the major challenges is to move from just being "respected" to being able to engage on a real level with the different "tribes". How churches do this arises from a deeper understanding of their surrounding cultures coupled with an ability to exegete the culture.

Understanding Culture

Christians have increasingly become aware of the need to engage with culture as part of Christian mission and theology.[12] And while there has been disagreement over whether popular culture affords new possibilities for evangelism or whether it's best to avoid it altogether, it is important for Christians to work hard at understanding their surrounding culture.

---

11. The suburb of Oran Park in the South West of Sydney is just one such example where all those infrastructure aspects were planned into the suburb well before any hole was dug.

12. Vanhoozer, *Everyday Theology*, 32.

Hence, the critical issue that drives a missional ecclesiology is the church's relationship to the culture in which it finds itself.

We've already established the problem for the church in trying to reclaim the idyllic notions of Christendom where the church held a central place in society. Using the theological insights of mission and exile and drawing together contemporary ideas from modern scholarship, we will outline a framework for understanding the relationship of church and culture.

It is necessary therefore to explore this notion of culture, what it is and how the church ought to engage with it.

Paul Hiebert defines culture as "the integrated system of learned patterns of behaviour, ideas and products characteristic of a society."[13]

In talking about society, we are referring to the institutional forms of organisation within which, and the norms or conventions by which a group of people live.[14] These norms can be thought of:

> . . . as commanding truths which define the 'shoulds' and 'should nots' of our experience and accordingly, the good and evil, the right and wrong, the appropriate and the inappropriate, the honourable and shameful . . . culture is a system of truth claims and moral obligations.[15]

One can think of culture as a lens through which a vision of life and social order is expressed, experienced and explored. It is, according to Vanhoozer, a "lived worldview", stemming from how one understands anthropology.[16] From anthropology we learn that culture is a way of life—everything that people do, say, have, make, think—learned and shared by members of a particular society.[17] All of these aspects which go towards everyday life signify something about the values and beliefs which shape culture.

In a sense, God created culture. That is, he created humanity with the capacity for creativity, communication, social interaction, for ruling over animals and the natural order (Gen 1:26-27)—all of this falls within our concept of culture. As humans created in the image of God, we have the capacity for thinking, reflecting, forming relationships with others, communicating with others, exercising power and authority. All these activities

13. Hiebert, *Cultural Anthropology*, 25.

14. Vanhoozer, *Everyday Theology*, 23.

15. Hunter, *Change the World*, 32-33.

16. Vanhoozer, *Everyday Theology*, 26.

17. Vanhoozer, *Everyday Theology*, 24.

are reflected in culture. Into this mix however comes sin with the Fall in Genesis 3. The Fall resulted in corruption of human nature and brought with it ongoing implications for mankind's relationship with God, with one another and the created order which now groans under the weight of sin (Rom 8:19-21). The cultural capacities which were a good and perfect part of the created order are now twisted and used for sinful ends. We see these effects both on an individual level but also at the collective and institutional level. Though we see the erosion of culture and society because of sin, the glorious message of the gospel is that God has taken the initiative to provide a way for sinful humanity to be reconciled to God its creator.

Thus, cultures must be understood theologically as mixed. That is, the very possibility of culture is a gift of God's grace, and the many good and positive things we find in the cultures of the world reflect the goodness of God the Creator. Nevertheless, every culture is affected profoundly by sin—both at an individual and institutional level.

The tendency towards the negative and sinful aspects of culture amidst the erosion of civil society (in terms of a gradual erosion of a sense of belonging for people) is being felt strongly as we follow the erosion of society in Britain and North America in the:

> . . . sliding toward a comprehensive relativism in which standards
> of good and bad, of right and wrong, are grounded in the opinions
> of individuals and left-wing groups. Tolerance has become abso-
> lute in a culture where anything goes. The exercise of discernment
> is frequently interpreted as an expression of judgmentalism.[18]

No less than 20 years ago, a Judeo-Christian worldview still held sway to some measure in reality and ethics. Now this perspective is ridiculed. Living together unmarried is a cultural given. To doubt that homosexuality should be promoted is labelled intolerant, divisive and homophobic. No one is talking about "Christophobia" as Christian views are mocked and scorned.

Gibbs notes the experience when it comes to how differences are now being challenged in a hyper-relativistic and pluralistic culture. Immigration has changed the fabric of Australian society, in many ways for the better. However, like North America we have struggled to make respectful and compassionate contacts with the influx of Muslim people, and others, to the point where there are concentrated pockets of different

---

18. Gibbs, *Rebirth*, 19.

people groups across Sydney. There is also, due to the ongoing threat of terrorism, an underlying fear of those who are immigrating legally or seeking asylum on our shores. The cultural and religious pluralism that surrounds us means that churches need to think about how they will respond to this constantly changing face of society. This is where churches take differing approaches to culture.

Christian Approaches to Culture

It's worth considering the way early Christians navigated their cultural contexts, since faith communities have always sought to engage the world with the gospel *kerygma*. Blake Hartung, in an insightful article dealing with faithful presence in a non-Christian world, argues that a combination of challenging social expectations, coupled with modelling an alternative vision of religion and community, whilst remaining faithful to their convictions, allowed the early church to live and participate in society in such a way that transformed both the early church and culture in which it found itself. In the ancient Mediterranean world, *religio* (the Latin ancestor of our word *religion*) was a collection of social practices thought to promote social cohesion and traditional values and therefore quite closely tied in with social and political life.[19]

Early Christianity didn't enjoy the same reputation with the Greco-Roman elites, who viewed it as a dangerous superstition characterized amongst other things by irrationality and an overzealous devotion to the divine.[20]

That the early Christians abstained from involving themselves in the civic *religio* showed an apparent disregard for their city, their people and ancestral traditions. This refusal to participate in their community's *religio* was deemed offensive to the pagan pluralism that bound the Roman Empire together.

Despite this opposition, the early church continued to grow. Hartung points out that this growth and organisation brought with it a new focus on charitable activities in areas such as food distribution, care for the sick, protection of orphans—aspects of life foreign to Greco-Roman *religio*.[21] It was Julian the Apostate in the late 4th century who began to imitate this,

19. Hartung, "Back to the Future," 16.
20. Hartung, "Back to the Future," 17.
21. Hartung, "Back to the Future," 17.

believing that pagans must "Christianize" their religion to make it more attractive to the masses.[22]

One of the features of *religio* is the non-separation of religious and secular spheres, whereby:

> Early Christians tried to walk a fine line: to declare their obedience to the emperor and their earthly citizenship in their place of residence, while resisting the daily public pressure to show support to these powers through sacrifices, libations and festivals.[23]

There is always the temptation to compromise in different ways, whether it be blending in or "accommodating" the culture. However Hartung helpfully reminds us that early Christianity was never just a system of ethics but first and foremost a proclamation of the gospel of Jesus. John Dickson has explored this issue in terms of the way in which early Christians engaged in mission. From detailed examination and exegesis of large sections of the Pauline letters, Dickson argues that the early church engaged in (and was expected to be involved in) mission at a series of levels. First, by way of partnership through financial assistance and intercession.[24] Then, in their own locale, they were to commend the gospel by mixing in society (ch. 8), adorning the gospel with honourable behaviour (ch. 9), and showing and telling the truth in public worship (esp. 1 Cor 14.20-25) and ad hoc conversations with outsiders (ch. 10).

In the larger mission of the gospel via partnership with Paul (see esp. Phil 1.3-5; 2 Cor 9.13), Dickson argues for a "two-dimensional view of mission": with apostolic heralds central to proclamation in mission, while congregations partnered with them in a variety of ways. That is, mission was promoted (as was alluded to above) by way of ethical and verbal apologetic, and financial assistance to those directly involved, and prayer.[25]

While there is disagreement with Dickson regarding his restriction of proclamation to recognized local evangelists who stand in continuity with the Isaianic herald tradition,[26] this isn't the concern of our scope. However, it is worth pointing out (as was seen in the treatment of 1 Peter), Dickson's proclamation-promotion concern means that mission is:

---

22. Hartung, "Back to the Future," 17.

23. Hartung, "Back to the Future," 18.

24. Dickson, *Mission-Commitment*, 178-227.

25. Dickson, *Mission-Commitment*, ix-x.

26. Dickson, *Mission Commitment*, 317.

The range of activities by which members of a conversion-desirous religion seek to promote their ways or beliefs to non-adherents.[27]

In other words, social integration with unbelieving society, whether that be in the way Peter exhorts his recipients to engage in an ethical apologetic, or spoken and unspoken promotion (1 Pet 3:1-7) or Paul's exhortation to the church in Thessalonica to, "make it your ambition to lead a quiet life, to mind your own business and to work with your hands, just as we told you, so that your daily life may win the respect of outsiders and so that you will not be dependent on anybody" (4:11-12, cf. Titus 2:3-10), can "provide outsiders with the opportunity to observe the godly "appearance" of the Christian community . . . and so be drawn to embrace the path to true piety."[28] In Paul's view, Christians were to be cognizant of the fact that they lived in full view of an unbelieving society and therefore needed to strive to adorn the gospel to those around them as they held out "the benefit of salvation to humankind."[29]

According to Dickson, such missionary thinking, including but not limited to the ethical apologetic, was a significant feature of the missionary outlook of various writings of the early church, from *The Letter of Aristeas* to the writings of Philo and Josephus.

It was a commitment to *kerygma* that drove how the early church interacted with the society around them. And though it proved a significant stumbling block to those around, for the early Christians their interactions with philosophical categories of Greco-Roman thought were always subservient to their faith in the incarnation, life, death and resurrection of Jesus. This allowed them to reject, appropriate, or completely rework the teachings of the ancient philosophers.[30] Hartung illustrates with the example of the Bishops at the Council of Nicaea who, when looking for language to describe the Father-Son relationship within the context of the Trinity relied on Greek philosophical terminology ("*ousia*") to aid their understanding. Even back then some Christians baulked at the use of the unbiblical term.

All this serves to highlight that although they may have been misunderstood, the early Christians didn't retreat into their own communities in the face of hostility. Instead, they faced their critics, defended themselves and even at times co-opted the culture of the day.

27. Dickson, *Mission-Commitment*, 257.

28. Dickson, *Mission-Commitment*, 259.

29. Dickson, *Mission-Commitment*, 291.

30. Hartung, "Back to the Future," 22.

In the face of critique and new questions it's important for pastors to engage with people in the community. There will be a tension in this but as Hartung notes:

> . . . this engagement was the impetus for some of the earliest Christian attempts to bring their Scripture, their kerygma, and their moral convictions into a comprehensive theological system . . . [and] offered a vision of Christian faith that was rational and all-encompassing, distinctly Christian, yet culturally engaged.[31]

As Western society has become more pluralistic and as Christians inhabit a largely non-Christian society; as our Judeo-Christian heritage finds itself under attack, whether that be aggressively or via subtle social pressures, rather than succumbing to modern views and standards, the church has to work out how to remain true to the faith once delivered to all the saints. This is where:

> The early church reminds us that to remain winsomely engaged with a non-Christian world, while remaining faithful to the gospel, requires resistance to the religios that seek our allegiance.[32]

Cultural Liturgies

This is where, according to James K. A. Smith, it is important to learn to read the practices of our culture and learn to understand and interpret the rituals we're immersed in.[33] Rather than just discerning the worldviews competing with the gospel, we need to look closely at, and even exegete, the places and sites of our modern culture.

Shopping malls for example, are cathedrals of consumerism that try to capture our loves and desires. In my previous context, it was being a citizen of "the Shire" (colloquially known as "God's country"), and the Cronulla beach and the lifestyle associated with that. In my current context it's the beach and lifestyle. Both captivate peoples' desires and reveal the idols of their hearts.

Both invite us into a visual set of routines and rituals that at their core, and in pretty covert ways, are trying to tell us that this is where satisfaction

---

31. Hartung, "Back to the Future," 23.

32. Hartung, "Back to the Future," 23.

33. Smith, *You are What You Love*, 40.

can be found. For example, Cronulla Surf Club produced weekly newsletters, in which the president of the club often had a message for members. Each message would always be signed off with the phrase, "where else would you rather be". This was, no doubt, in relation to the community of Cronulla Surf Life Saving Club (SLSC) but also the beach itself. We're captivated by the lifestyle, and we become consumers in places like the beach or the local mall where our hearts are captured by cultural liturgies that pull us toward a different story, "a rival understanding of the good life".[34]

Smith points to stadiums, but it is not just limited to that. Even various aspects of popular culture offer an "embodied visual mode of evangelism that *attracts* us . . . a gospel whose power is beauty and speaks to our deepest desires"[35] of what is true, good and beautiful. Indeed Chapter 7 will endeavour to show how we can bring that liturgical lens to various micro-cultures as we bring the gospel to bear on this envisioned "good life".

Understanding these sociological and cultural challenges in this respect means showing a concern for sub-cultures. Vanhoozer notes that Martin Heidegger, the existentialist philosopher, believed that concern or care ("*sorge*") is what makes us distinctly human; one could phrase it as: you shall know them by what drives them. As he unpacks culture within the nature of our everyday world, he points to Paul Tillich, a leading theologian of culture, who said that the best way to understand a particular culture or even epoch is to discover its greatest anxiety (i.e., the focus of a negative concern) and its greatest hope (i.e., the focus of what Tillich called "ultimate concern," or simply "religion").[36] We begin to understand others and groups of others, then, when we begin to understand what concerns them and why.[37]

This is why I wanted to interview the ministers of the churches as well as gain a better understanding of the culture in which my ministry was located at the time, by interviewing the "gatekeepers". I spent time speaking with the local cultural gatekeepers (café owner, community figures, long-term residents, Shire councillor) in an effort to understand different micro-cultures and the deep-seated beliefs and worldviews that drive them. Essentially I was able to confirm what I had thought for some time about what makes people tick. I gained valuable insights

34. Smith, *You are What You Love*, 47.

35. Smith, *You are What you Love*, 43.

36. Vanhoozer, *Everyday Theology*, loc. 232.

37. Vanhoozer, *Everyday Theology*, loc. 254.

into questions around their perceptions of church; why people think they don't need Jesus; what's so good about life now, and have we as the church just grossly undersold eternal life?

Changing worldviews and plausibility structures alongside the incredible shift in our nation to a post-Christian standpoint in a relatively short space of time, means we need to think carefully about our responses to questions like the ones above. Change like this, with different worldviews bringing their own sets of challenges to classical Christianity, has confronted God's people in every age and in every place. Indeed, there have been numerous responses throughout history: retreat and batten down the hatches (so to speak); conflict and the mindset that the world can be conquered for Christ; change the culture; or embrace the culture (which can and has led some churches down dangerous pathways whereby they become all but unrecognisable).

Much has been written in an effort to help the church come to grips with the culture in a society where the church has become increasingly marginalized. One way is contextualisation.

Contextualisation: From Niebuhr to Keller

Contextualisation is taking into consideration the cultural context in which we are seeking to communicate the gospel. In other words, it is the process of making the gospel and the church as much at home as possible in a given cultural context.

One of the most significant theological and missiological treatments in the 20th century was Niebuhr's *Christ and Culture*. His framework sought to categorize the ways Christians have related to culture throughout history. His basic typology, which has become widely recognized in the fields of mission and ecclesiology, is that churches can adopt one of five stances with respect to culture: against culture, of culture, above culture, in paradox with culture and transforming culture.[38] It's worth pointing out that in some cases, more than one of Niebuhr's categories may apply at the same time and that various people and movements travel in and out of the territories and meanings of the categories in real life.[39]

Often Christians have tended to see the culture as a Christian culture within which some secular people live. In reality the changes are

38. Niebuhr, *Christ and Culture*, 39-44.

39. Carson, *Gagging of God*, 405-6.

more profound. Christians must see themselves as believers inhabiting a secular culture.

Along those lines in the US context, James Davison Hunter has noted shortcomings among the three main Christian traditions. In his research, he summarized the approaches of the Evangelical, Liberal and Anabaptist traditions as three paradigms of engagement: the evangelical approach as "defense against" the culture, the liberal approach as "relevance to" the culture and the Anabaptist approach as "purity from" the culture. Historically, the Anabaptist approach stemmed from a desire to want to create the city of God then and there in some German cities. Their failure to do that led to a total pull back and separation from the world. While each of these paradigms captures something important to the experience, life, identity and witness of church, the concern of each does speak to authentic biblical concerns.[40] Even so, as Hunter points out, each has its own failings: the desire for relevancy can easily see distinctiveness abandoned; defensiveness can sometimes come across as aggressive or confrontational, meaning non-believers are more likely to switch off; the desire to retain purity can lead to almost total disengagement and withdrawal from the public arena. The end result is that "none seems to be a fully adequate way of making sense of or pursuing faithfulness in our world."[41]

In more modern times, particularly in America there has been the tendency (largely through the political spectrum) to want to use Christians in politics to take over (or take back) America. Hunter shows how the dominant Christian strategy in the United States, when it comes to changing the culture, has historically been to focus on the worldview of individuals but also to seek change in the political realm. This thinking stems from the assumption that "the essence of culture is found in the hearts and minds of individuals".[42]

Hunter postulates that since culture is formed by institutions and the elite that influence them, Christians in America have placed a high idealism on changing the culture with an astonishing hope, placed particularly by Christian conservatives, in politics. This is to the point where in lobbying for and supporting one particular candidate, Christians can, he says quoting one activist, "do more than just elect a president. We seek to heal

---

40. Hunter, *Change the World*, 223.

41. Hunter, *Change the World*, 223-4.

42. Hunter, *Change the World*, 6.

a nation."[43] This largely stems from a misunderstanding of the Kingdom of God. As we saw in the previous chapter, the Kingdom of God is ushered in through new birth and faith in Jesus (Matt 12:28; Luke 17:21; 21:31; John 3:3, 5). It is also, as Jesus pointed to, a realm of righteousness, justice and blessing: even here in this world, in that we experience some of that now but not yet fully as we await its final consummation (Matt 5:12, 20; 6:33; 7:21; 19:23-24). The issue for Christians is working out, when it comes to the relationship of Christianity and culture, in what time and place will these things happen? One view is that Christians can usher in that aspect of the Kingdom by assuming positions of influence and power (as explored by Hunter) to the extent that, as Geerhadus Vos points out, the institutional church with enough influence can bring that justice and blessing to bear by controlling society through political power.

In his book *Awaiting the King*, James K. A. Smith asserts that the church has no part in bringing in the Kingdom; it's Jesus who ushers it in, for "our teleology is an eschatology: a hope for kingdom come that arrives with the return of the risen King."[44] Indeed, in an age where the Christian worldview can no longer be assumed, it's incumbent upon Christians to understand that God's mission is completed with the coming of the Kingdom of God into the world. In a sense we are watching that play out as we engage in mission (Smith says that too often Christians are Pelagian in their thinking about this). Foster points out the mistake that's made is in thinking that the church's function is to extend, build, spread or grow the Kingdom. Usually understood in expansionist terms, the church's mission (as was mentioned earlier in this chapter) isn't actually described in these terms.[45] A cursory glance of the New Testament shows us that the Kingdom is something to be received; something we enter into.[46] Interestingly George Hunsberger, in exploring how the people of God are called and sent to "re-present" the reign of God, notes that the announcement of this reign "nowhere includes an invitation to go out and build it, nor to extend it . . . The words most often used evoke . . . a very different missional identity and engagement."[47]

---

43. Hunter, *Change the World*, 127.

44. Smith, *Awaiting the King*, 10.

45. Foster, Unpublished DMin Dissertation, 106.

46. Luke 18:17, 24-25, 29-30; Luke 12:32, 6:20.

47. Hunsberger, *Between Gospel and Culture*, 93.

In summary, we are expecting too much if we think that getting particular people into positions of power will bring about a change in culture. Hunter sees that if Christians and indeed the church is to be effective, they must "operate with as much grace and forgiveness as possible because failure to use power rightly is unavoidable."[48] There is a gospel way of thinking about power and a better way of engaging with the world. Thus, Hunter cautions us towards new ways that Christians ought to think and speak in public that are actually 'decoupled' from the political sphere.[49] He examines briefly the social power exercised by Jesus in the Gospels, noting the "rejection of status and reputation and the privilege that accompanies them".[50] We see this throughout the Gospels, but particularly in the Lucan narrative in the way Jesus interacted with those deemed to be outsiders from the community of faith (Luke 5, 7, cf. John 4).

As a modern movement, Hunter says that Christianity has actually been ineffective in creating and changing culture. In the third essay in his book, he outlines in practice a model of power that derives from Christ's life and teaching, which enables the Christian faith to flourish and for the church to indeed be effective in the impact it can have on the surrounding culture. Hunter calls this a Theology of Faithful Presence.

Christians need to understand the unique and evolving character of our times. Because the multiplicity of challenges and the dizzying complexity of their causes make this modern world at times so confounding, Hunter says this "historical moment in which we find ourselves requires a rethink of the particular challenges to Christian witness if we're to engage the world with integrity."[51]

He outlines a number of challenges: pluralism, dissolution (where our most basic assumptions about reality have been deconstructed), and communications technologies. These go right to the core of Christians' ability to live out their faith with integrity, let alone be effective in their witness in the world, prompting him to ask: "How is faithfulness possible? . . . And what might be a way forward?"[52]

This is where contextualisation enters the discussion, the purpose of which is to communicate the gospel; not to accommodate every idea in a

---

48. Hunter, *Change the World*, 184.
49. Hunter, *Change the World*, 186.
50. Hunter, *Change the World*, 189.
51. Hunter, *Change the World*, 199.
52. Hunter, *Change the World*, 213.

culture, nor to demonise everything in it either. As Timothy Keller put it in his excellent treatment in *Center Church*:

> To contextualize with balance and successfully reach people in a culture, we must both enter the culture sympathetically and respectfully (similar to drilling) and confront the culture where it contradicts biblical truth (similar to blasting).[53]

Keller outlines how contextualisation is a process consisting of three overlapping parts: (1) entering the culture, (2) challenging the culture, and (3) appealing to the listeners. Entering the culture involves immersing yourself:

> ... in the questions, hopes, and beliefs of the culture so you can give a biblical, gospel-centered response to its questions ... Ultimately, the most important source for learning will be the hours and hours spent in close relationships with people, listening to them carefully.[54]

Part of considering our culture involves determining its dominant worldviews or belief systems, because contextualized gospel ministry should affirm the beliefs of the culture wherever it can be done with integrity.

Keller outlines looking for two kinds of beliefs: what he calls "A" beliefs, (beliefs people already hold, that, because of God's common grace, roughly correspond to some parts of biblical teaching); and "B" or "defeater" beliefs (beliefs of the culture that lead listeners to find some Christian doctrines implausible or overtly offensive). "B" beliefs contradict Christian truth directly at points we may call "B" doctrines.[55]

Contextualisation's approach first seeks to affirm our culture's "A" beliefs, and then use these beliefs to challenge people to accept the "B" doctrines. Keller further explains:

> Every culture (including our own) can readily grasp part of the truth but not all of it. And we know that biblical truth, because it is from God, is coherent and *consistent* with itself ... The confrontation occurs because every culture is profoundly inconsistent, conforming to some biblical truths but not to others. If those in a particular culture hold certain 'A' beliefs, they are inconsistent not to hold 'B' beliefs because the Scriptures, as the revealed truth of

---

53. Keller, *Center Church*, 119.

54. Keller, *Center Church*, 121.

55. Keller, *Center Church*, 123.

God, are always consistent. These inconsistencies reveal the points where a culture is vulnerable to confrontation.[56]

The letter of first Peter helps us think about this within the context of mission and our identity as strangers in a strange land. In our earlier treatment, we saw how the dominant metaphor of aliens and strangers was not just aimed at the situation of the original recipients to help them understand how to live as those who had been blessed with new birth into a living hope, and who are therefore, "a chosen race, a royal priesthood, a holy nation" (1 Pet 2:9) but also helps the church think more deeply about what it looks like in our post-Christian context.

In a helpful essay, *Soft Difference*, Miroslav Volf picks up on this notion of Christian existence and what it means to accommodate to existing social structures while being different, as those called to "proclaim the mighty acts of him who called you out of darkness into his marvellous light" (1 Pet 2:9). He puts it this way:

> Christian difference is . . . not an insertion of something new into the old from the outside, but a bursting out of the new precisely within the proper space of the old.[57]

Thus, his assertion is that first Peter doesn't mandate a change of social structures; instead the mission of Christians as they seek to live out their difference, is a *soft difference*: seeking to win others without pressure or manipulation.[58] That is, living out our identity in such a way that "one joins inseparably the belief in the truth of one's own convictions with a respect for the convictions of others" to the point where we recognize, along with Volf, that:

> there are numerous ways of accepting, rejecting, subverting or transforming various aspects of culture which itself is a complex pattern of symbols, beliefs values, practices, organisations that are partly congruent with one another and partly contradictory.[59]

This is why Keller's approach to contextualisation is so helpful. With the authority of the Bible we allow one part of the culture—along with the Bible—to critique another part. The persuasive force comes from basing

---

56. Keller, *Center Church*, 124.

57. Volf. "Soft Difference," 21.

58. Volf, "Soft Difference," 24.

59. Volf, "Soft Difference," 27.

our critique on something we can affirm within the culture.[60] In fact, from our qualitative research findings presented in the next chapter, our analysis will point to ways forward that adopt some of what has been said; recognising the rich diversity within any given culture and the multiple ways in which the gospel can speak into it faithfully.

In a similar vein to Keller's "A" and "B" beliefs held by our culture and the strategy to interact with them, Hunter uses the terms "Affirmation" and "Antithesis" as a way of relating to the culture around us.

When it comes to affirmation, we recognize biblically that everything God created is good, and that there is goodness, truth and beauty to be found in our fallen world. Paul affirms this in 1 Timothy 4, but often the pendulum of Christian witness has swung in the other direction to the detriment of gospel proclamation (captured particularly in the "purity from" stance).

We will see how there are elements within the culture of the suburban coastal context that can be celebrated and indeed how the gospel can speak deeply into those aspects. Hunter captures it in this way:

> The qualities nonbelievers possess as well as the accomplishments they achieve may not be righteous in an eschatological sense, but they should be celebrated all the same because they are gifts of God's grace . . . there is a world that God created that is shared in common by believers and non-believers alike.[61]

As such there are points of contact and overlap: points of common cause in the pursuit of beauty, justice, peace and wellbeing between the Christian community and others. These have been identified for the purposes of more intentional engagement. What we will also see are the "ways in" for the gospel message when it comes to points of vulnerability, or "touchpoints" of the culture that we may not have considered, particularly in relation to some of the cultural difficulties that we find ourselves facing e.g., relationship breakdown, addiction, the reach of social media and other technologies.

Often it is our engagement with our culture in this way that provides churches with the opportunity to proclaim an element of the Kingdom which is to come. Our world in putting its hope in created things and everything to which they aspire, is but a poor imitation of the final heavenly

---

60. Keller, *Center Church*, 125.
61. Hunter, *Change the World*, 232.

community. Hence while there's much we can affirm, the church is always a community of resistance and therefore must model its alternative in the way it exists within different spheres of social life.[62] Indeed, "as a natural expression of its passion to honour God in all things and to love our neighbour as ourselves, the church and its people will challenge all structures that dishonour God."[63] This stance, what Hunter labels 'antithesis', isn't negational for it requires a commitment to the modern world in such a way that envisions it differently. Instead, the church must always oppose the structures that undermine human flourishing and offer creative and constructive alternatives in shining the light on a better way, "guided by devotion to the beloved community."[64]

As this happens, it is possible to show that Jesus offers that better way, in proclaiming this good news to call people from the dominion of darkness into the Kingdom of Jesus. As people are rescued from the power of sin and drawn to love and follow Jesus by virtue of his death and resurrection, this has tremendous implications. Indeed, while we've articulated that the atonement can be a helpful model for the church and mission, the implications of Jesus' death and resurrection for God's people, "has enormous implications for every aspect of life."[65]

Thus for Newbigin, when the church realizes its distinctive stance, it is driven to share the gospel.[66] In doing so the church will adjust to its cultural context while guarding against conforming to the cultural context.[67] Hence the tension of a delicate balancing act which Newbigin described as a concept of "challenging relevance",

> that when the gospel only challenges but does not become part of the culture, it leads to irrelevance; and when the gospel becomes conformed to culture without challenging it, it leads to syncretism.[68]

In this setting, Newbigin's words some nine years later seem as relevant as ever:

62. Hunter, *Change the World*, 235.

63. Hunter, *Change the World*, 235.

64. Hunter, *Change the World*, 236.

65. Hunter, *Change the World*, 236.

66. Newbigin, "Evangelism in the City," 4.

67. Nikolajsen, "Beyond Christendom," 374.

68. Newbigin, *Foolishness*, 7.

The mystery of the gospel is not entrusted to the church to be buried in the ground. It is entrusted to the church to be risked in the change and interchange of the spiritual commerce of humanity. It belongs not to the church but to the one who is both head of the church and head of the cosmos. It is within his power and grace to bring to its full completion that long-hidden purpose, the secret of which has been entrusted to the church in order that it may become the open manifestation of the truth to all the nations.[69]

In conclusion, the notion of living within and engaging effectively with the prevailing culture has emerged as a significant topic of conversation amongst Evangelicals in Australia in recent years. This has given shape to the concept that Christians now ought to be thinking of themselves as exiles in a post-Christian culture. We have already shown how the theme of exiles forces churches to re-think how they perceive themselves, how they might be perceived in their suburbs and therefore how that changes the way they engage with the surrounding culture.

This presents a challenge for churches to discover how our community life can be a distinctive witness. This perspective requires an intentional process of discipleship in their churches, intentional community engagement, and a robust understanding of what faithful presence looks like—each of which will be fleshed out as ways forward in Chapter 7. The upshot is that through a reasonable understanding of culture and how to do contextualisation well, Christians can be equipped to live for Christ in a secular world. This is especially critical in seeking to reach the emerging generations who are influenced by an increasingly post-Christendom environment.

69. Newbigin, *Open Secret*, 189.

6

Attitudes & Aspirations: What the Research Revealed

Methodological Considerations

WE ESTABLISHED IN OUR Biblical Theological survey in chapter 3 the scope and nature of the exile within the framework of salvation history, and how the Apostle Peter applies that to the situation of the scattered Christians throughout Asia Minor in the 1st century early church.

In both cases it is clear that the situation of the exile for Israel and the situation for the Christians of the dispersion in first Peter could be construed as similar: a small remnant which found themselves in a wider situation that ignores and at worst belittles or even persecutes their faith.

The easy identification of church, society and nation that has served Western Christians for centuries is becoming increasingly difficult in our modern secular society. In this post-Christian context, the church has lost much power and influence—a loss of moral power says Smith-Christopher that has led to a loss of authority which have lain behind various attempts to persuade our secular society to consider different trajectories.[1] This makes exile "a radically sobering diagnosis for the present reality of Christian existence."[2] It is, therefore, by extension, the situation in which church communities find themselves in this post-Christian part of the

1. Smith-Christopher, Biblical Theology of Exile, 191.
2. Smith-Christopher, Biblical Theology of Exile, 191.

21st century. Christians find themselves in a culture in this Western and western-influenced world that no longer shares their many basic cultural assumptions. It is a culture that still owes its foundation, strength and remaining moral fibre to Christian influence, although it has forgotten where visions of cultural mores such as justice, human rights and tolerance came from. As Mark Sayers puts it:

> The rise of a post-Christian society, alongside declining numbers of those who practice biblical faith, combined with a corresponding weaking of Christian influence, has created an anxious mood. This mood can range from a sense of defeat to feeling vulnerability to a desire to retreat into a religious Refuge . . . Our fears are usually connected to the boogeyman we call secularism.[3]

I designed my research to look at what is going on now, both in churches, but also in the suburbs in which they're located, because churches in coastal areas are in many ways like the situation of exile. That is, there is little or no engagement with the church, and while some might be located in a geographically central or significant place in the suburb, they are (as I established back in chapter 2) culturally on the fringes. In fact alongside the collapse of Christendom and the shift from post-modernity with the desires for authenticity, autonomy and affirmation coupled with gnostic undertones, its in this moment that humans are longing for "the Good Life" (my final chapter will unpack this more). People long more for community: to be known and to be loved, and the failure of secularism to deliver is leaving a gaping hole in our society.

Thus, the questions that were asked of both churches and community figures (as can be seen in appendices 3 & 5) were designed with several aims in mind. Largely, to gain a snapshot of this cultural moment in time showing that churches in suburban coastal contexts are in an exile-like situation. The interviews I conducted with the ministers and the Cronulla locals were designed to look at "what is" with the words of those who are at the coalface. For example, in my interviews with the 9 churches we looked at the nature of each church's relationship with the culture around them. We explored issues of each church's strength and weakness. We explored their programs of outreach done throughout the week and the types of ministries they run in order to engage with their communities. We talked about the efforts their church had historically made to understand their community, as well as the extent to which the ministers had sought to understand their respective

3. Sayers, *Disappearing Church*, 19.

community. In an effort to gain an idea of where congregation members were at and the cultural DNA of the church, each minister was asked about the extent to which they think their congregation is able to engage those who aren't Christians, or who haven't set foot in the church in a long time (the 'de-churched'), with the gospel. The question on how well each church had engaged in the past with the suburb particularly was designed to draw out each minister's thoughts on where they perceive their communities to be, and the changes they have seen in the time of their tenure.

It's worth noting at this point, I had intended to gain access to locals in the other coastal contexts as we did with Cronulla. This would have been ideal. However, COVID prevented this from occurring. I therefore used the interviews with what I called the 'gatekeepers' at Cronulla along with the historical-sociological research to show that many of the aspects of lifestyle in Cronulla are largely typical of a beachside suburb. Indeed, phenomenological research allows us to some extent to apply specifics in a universal way.

For example, just in the Sydney area alone there are 7,600 young "surf lifesavers in training" (Nippers) who gather at fifteen surf life saving clubs in the months of September to April. According to Surf Life Saving Sydney, that number makes up a third of the overall membership for the Sydney branch alone. Of those 7,600, one-fifth of those children aged 5-13 years are part of four clubs along the stretch of beach within the Cronulla Parish.[4] Since culture is a way of life for a group of people—behaviours, beliefs, values and symbols they accept, generally without thinking about them, and because they are passed along by communication and imitation from one generation to the next, the culture that is built into the micro-culture of surf lifesaving in that community represents the larger cultural attitude towards commitment, community leisure and family priorities.

Though its important to point out from the results gathered from the interviews with ministers that there are various cultural differences between (and even within) the Northern Beaches, the South, the 'Coal Coast' and what we could call the city beaches, there are also a number of similarities as we will see in the next chapter—the most common being that almost all can be considered destination suburbs. It's the idea that people will do everything they can to settle down in these suburbs whether they're at a family stage of life or in their retirement. There are also cultural differences when it comes to sociology and demographics. However, there are also cultural

---

4. The four clubs are Cronulla, North Cronulla, Elouera and Wanda.

nuances in these coastal contexts which all point to a long-term, long-held culture that reflects the desire for "the good life" and what it looks like to "belong". Again, the questions asked of the ministers of the nine churches and also those within what the writer deemed to be significant spheres of influence of the Cronulla community reflected this.

Thus, the questions were designed in such a way as to show what the current situation is, so churches can be equipped to plan what to do with the circumstances they currently face in their post-Christian exilic contexts.

Earlier in this work, I outlined three goals to understand the challenges that churches in suburban and/or urban coastal contexts face in Sydney and suggest some pathways that may assist churches in their particular suburban coastal contexts. The main goal is to (where necessary) help churches shift their church life to a mindset that enables them to bring gospel impact to their community and the underlying microcultures, such that, where they may have historically struggled, they become equipped to be more missionally-focused, as well as encouraged to reconsider their approach to ministry planning. The aim is that this planning may bring significant, gospel-based, long-term impact on individual church members, on the community life of the church, and therefore, the in lives of non-believers, and bring blessing to their suburbs, growth to Christ's church, and glory to God.

At this point, I want to reiterate that this research was borne out of a pastoral desire. My methodology allowed me to explore some of my hypotheses having spent nearly a decade of pastoral ministry at my church. These hypotheses included: the secular hedonism associated with the culture and lifestyle of a beachside suburb like Cronulla as a reason for why people are disengaged from church. Also, that churches often find themselves on the cultural fringe, meaning that people in these communities have little or nothing to do with church except on seasonal days of Christmas and Easter and in those significant life moments of baptisms, weddings or funerals. Though Cronulla Anglican enjoyed an iconic status within the broader community and was well-regarded by the population of Cronulla, it (and other churches) doesn't always hold the position of esteem that a community like the Surf Life Saving Club perhaps does. These hypotheses coupled with the results of our conversations shows that people aren't stridently anti-church. Many interactions the writer had over ten years revealed people sympathetic to Christianity but resistant to the call of the gospel on their lives with Jesus as King. The overall hypothesis was that these are reflective of a post-Christian secular culture where people are in pursuit of the fruits of a Kingdom without a King. This is why some churches struggle to engage effectively with the suburb. And while rebellion and refusal to give allegiance to Jesus as King, alone, does not explain this ongoing tension it did lead to questions of why the church no longer resonates with people in this context especially the younger generations.

The goal, therefore, was to gain a picture of how well or poorly churches have adapted to the changing Sydney landscape; what ministries have been tried in order to reach the unchurched of their community; what churches have done or are doing to facilitate a shift in the mindset of their members from attractional to missional ecclesial life; and various approaches and strategies thriving and struggling Christian churches have used to connect with their communities. Furthermore, we asked to what extent sustained cultural exegesis through the use of current census and/or National Church Life Survey data, along with demographic studies, have allowed a church to have a positive and significant impact in the life of their suburb. We sought to gain an overall picture of the different ministries that churches along the beaches of Sydney and the Northern Illawarra region have tried at different points over the last 20 years, as they have sought to engage their suburbs with the gospel. Having developed a big picture of the way these churches have operated in these suburbs, and armed with some current resources, we will be better placed to suggest further areas of exploration for churches as they seek to better engage with people in these suburban beachside contexts.

It is important to reiterate that those churches chosen were ones located with the beach and Surf Life Saving clubs in close proximity. The reason for this is because culturally, Surf Life Saving Clubs tend to have an important presence within the community. More significant is the impact that the Nippers culture has had and continues to have in the life of these suburbs and upon church life and ministry, both internally and externally.

My research also involved, interviews with key "cultural gatekeepers" of the Cronulla community. Those interviewed included a Sutherland Shire Councillor, an influential small-business owner, the former President of Cronulla Surf Life Saving Club, and a long-term Cronulla resident. This was done to develop a cohesive account of people's perceptions of their suburb and the place of Christian churches in these areas.

In order to develop a picture of the churches and the suburban context in which they minister, I was able to observe aspects like the demography of the suburbs, the physical setting of the churches, and even interactional patterns. This is important, since the task of observation involved allowed me to look at as many details as possible in particular settings.[5]

The basis for much of this research is what some researchers refer to as an 'interpretive paradigm'. This recognizes that the social world (for our purposes, the suburban/urban coastal contexts in which churches are located) is "local, temporally and historically situated, fluid, context specific, and shaped in conjunction with the researcher."[6] The goals, as articulated by Carol Bailey, involved empathetic understanding of the participants' day-to-day experiences and an increased awareness of the multiple meanings given to the routine and problematic events by those in the setting.[7] In the case of this research (questions used of both groups can be found in Appendices 3 and 5), the questions were designed to gain a picture of the strengths and weaknesses of each church's ministry and the cultural and demographic challenges that churches face. However, importantly within this, specific questions were then asked along the lines of community engagement, cultural exegesis and the impact of extra-curricular activities on church life with a special emphasis on the micro-cultures in suburban coastal contexts and Surf Life Saving Clubs in particular. In interviewing the "cultural gatekeepers", a similar goal applied as per Bailey above. But further, there is a recognition that for those in the community, (and it is helpful for churches to reflect on and understand this), there are socially significant meanings attached to their world. Like a nation's flag—which could either be thought of as a mix of different coloured materials sewn together in some consistent pattern, or a complex web of socially reflective emotions, symbolism and ideals—so communities and their culture are in many ways like the latter. This is what I sought to understand.

The cultural mosaic that not only gives the beaches their distinctiveness but also belies a complexity that lies beneath the surface meant that the interviews carried out required a mix of structured and unstructured questions within them as, more often than not, observations made by the interviewees would lead us to explore other applicable aspects of either church life or community life.

5. Ammerman, *Studying Congregations*, 199.

6. Guba and Lincoln, "Competing Paradigms," 109.

7. Bailey, *Qualitative Field Research*, 53.

Results

The churches interviewed were of particular sizes—a mixture of larger and smaller, and, while I was specifically interested in Anglican churches, the results also included a Baptist church in close geographic proximity to the beach.

The interviews yielded congregation timelines which have proved to be useful in understanding how these churches have situated themselves culturally and socially in their local context. These have proven to be important for uncovering links between external demographic, cultural, and organisational shifts and even internal stresses and strains experienced by the churches.[8]

'A' Church

The Senior Minister at 'A' Church has been in the role for three years. The staff team comprises the Senior Minister, an Assistant Minister and a Children's Worker. (Before the impact of COVID-19 they also had a two-day a week Missions Pastor). The role of the Missions Pastor was mainly geared towards encouraging the church to build a more intentional culture of mission in and around the suburb. Out of that role, they developed a particular ministry initiative which they call 'the Hub': seeking to use their space/building to "bless" the surrounding community. (One of the identified needs of the area is that when it comes to community spaces the suburb is particularly space-poor.) With the parish spanning five suburbs, the space-poor issue for the community was identified as an opportunity for the church. Within that, the church had the foresight to acquire the old multi-purpose RSL (Returned Servicemen's League) club building with future growth prospects in mind.

Having a Missions Pastor under the "purpose-driven" model of church enabled them to push deeply into mission, having acquired the premises. Having a key group of lay people within the church with a strong missional focus also helped in that they saw the vision for acquiring the premises and what that could mean for ministry and mission in the future. On the flipside, it was pointed out that there has been a cost to setting up a shared space they called 'the Hub' in terms of a diversion of limited resources. Even so, the establishment of this 'Hub' within their

8. Ammerman, *Studying Congregations*, 209

facilities has allowed them to partially set it aside and make it available to various surrounding community groups for one-off events (e.g., Not For Profit organisations or creative groups).

'A' Church is one of the few evangelical churches in the area and it has benefited from a strong missional heritage. They also enjoy good proximity to the geographical centre with the local cafés (a strong local café scene) and an excellent building facility. Their building is an old RSL club: a large double-storey building that, in the words of the Senior Minister, is a flexible ministry space. This means they're not bound as if they occupied a classic Anglican church building (or chapel).

The church comprises a congregational mix that is suitably reflective of the surrounding culture. It is a multi-site church with a smaller building and congregation situated in the next suburb, about 5 minutes' drive away. What is interesting here is that the main church is situated in a suburb with a smaller population (about a third of the size of the suburb next door). 10 to 20% of their members come from outside the main parish boundary.

Alongside the normal challenges, 'A' Church has the ongoing challenge of remaining outsider-focused, whilst being the warm open place to which people can invite their friends. The suburb has that mix of new arrivals versus hardened (long-term) locals. As is the case in many of these beachside contexts, there are strong local bonds that people feel within the area. This can sometimes permeate through to become a part of church culture.

An observation of the National Church Life Survey[9] data shows the challenge of significant groups such as those who we earlier classified as "the Nones": "I'm spiritual, but organized religion is evil." The Senior Minister described them as the "I know God, I don't need Jesus to know God because I've got my spirituality." A proportion of people in that area identify with the new-age spiritual focus which they've identified and tried to connect with. Interestingly, the results of the National Church Life Survey (from here referred to as NCLS), as well as equivalent government data, show that their

9. The National Church Life Survey is a world leader in research focused on connecting churches and their communities. Through rigorous and thoughtful research, it aims to examine wellbeing, spirituality and church health. As part of a nationally coordinated survey Anglican churches in Sydney participate in the five-yearly National Church Life Survey. Cooperating denominations include Catholics, Anglicans and other Protestants. The results of the survey enable churches to compare different areas of ministry with other churches locally and even nationally. The results allow for the sharing of practical resources to help churches engage in a more focused and intentional way with their communities.

local area has one of the highest concentrations of artists/creative types. This sub-culture that was largely unreached by the church could be observed in the culture and the events that are held within the community. There is also an historical anti-authoritarianism and anti-institutionalism which has impacted upon how they have approached mission. Indeed, it has forced them to grapple with issues like, in the Senior Minister's words:

> how much of the gospel . . . can you not compromise . . . how much can the gospel reach into a certain space before the gospel actually has to push against something? At some point you've got to pop the polite bubble and [at] some point you've got to go, 'we can go so far culturally, but at certain points, the gospel should change you and the gospel should mean you don't keep going down a certain path.'

Alongside the usual outreach church-based activities common among the churches we interviewed (playgroup, youth and children's ministry, Christmas and Easter gatherings), they have their regular ministry programs plus a few one-off events, and mission events combined with their 'Hub' ministry. These pre-existing structures enable them to build bridges from the community into church. For example, this church is able, through their existing children's ministry, to utilize Christmas as something to which families can be invited. Children's ministry in Term 4 is shaped towards Christmas. Two seasons a year of evangelistic courses has seen contacts from the playgroup and children's ministry bridged from those groups into regular Sunday gatherings.

'A' church uses Christmas and Easter as "missional opportune moments." Their major missional event surrounds Christmas, where the church has run the local Community Carols for the last ten years. Easter has given them the opportunity to run a 'sourdough and wine night' with a gospel explanation attached to that. They have also run the popular gingerbread house-making at Christmas. Post-Christmas they have run a summer series that invites people in the community to ask their questions about Christianity. The subsequent Sunday Bible teaching is based on those "common questions". During COVID-19, they tried a "love your street" initiative, as a way of caring for those who were shut in during the lockdowns in NSW.

Because the main church has a strong mission heritage, regular mission weeks have been a feature of the life of 'A' church as well as intentional time spent in prayer for the surrounding community; there is a practice of "prayer walks"[10] as a way to better understand the suburb.

'A' church has people in the congregation who are members of the local Surf Life Saving Club (SLSC). Up until this year they leveraged their existing relationship with the local SLSC to run a summer mission across four weeks in January—similar to the Scripture Union Beach Missions that occur up and down the NSW coastline. Their approach was to focus more on the young adults (similar to the Scripture Union "Theos" missions as opposed to family missions). The Senior Minister explains how during two years of this approach:

> . . . the first year we had perfect weather . . . lots of visitors and high attendance to the café, but in the second year, it rained all weekend, and it was terrible, terrible weather and we had hardly anyone, but the second year was probably better than the first in terms of local, missional contacts . . .

The suburb displays a strong sense of a village atmosphere. This was an important theme to emerge here and with other contexts, seen in the number of local newspapers/publications. One such publication, titled simply with the postcode of the suburb, highlights how something like a postcode can shape a sense of belonging for people, like the 2230 postcode for Cronulla which has contributed towards that "Shire" identity. The Senior Minister pointed out that people give their area a name that comes from a place of "aspiration". Again, as with many of these suburban coastal contexts, there's a desirability and an ambition that goes hand-in-hand with living in these areas.

One of the challenges facing 'A' Church (and which was also observed in the interviews with other pastors), is the aspirational element which is often a cultural feature connected to the beach and to coastline. There is a struggle to connect with those who've geared their lives towards that

---

10. Prayer walking is the practice of praying on location, a type of intercessory prayer that involves walking to or near a particular place while praying. It's something that can be done at an individual level but is a practice that in recent times churches have adopted. Praying in this way can help one observe what's happening in their neighbourhood. Karina Kreminski observes this as one way in which "we can function as cultural exegetes of our surroundings". You find out where different sub-cultures gather, who the locals are. It can lead to interactions and conversations. She says, "the more I walk around my neighbourhood praying, the more attached I get ot the place . . . This teaches me that I am tangibly connected to my neighbourhood in a very real way and reminds me . . . that the Spirit is present in my neighbourhood" (Kreminiski 2018, 185).

lifestyle—what he calls the "relaxed coastal types". The added pressure, which poses a challenge for churches in these areas, on top of connecting with the relaxed types, is how to help people in churches break free of the non-committal culture that has seeped into the church culture; that notion of: "if I come to church, I might come to church but if I don't it's no big deal." The attendance struggle is not particular to beachside suburban churches but perhaps it's exacerbated by the relaxed coastal culture.

Combine this challenge with the difference between those in the suburb on weekdays (usually residents or workers) to those there on the weekends (most beachside suburbs attract a lot of weekend visitors to the area). Thus, part of the challenge when it comes to working on contextualisation, is working out where you're going to pour your missional energy, and working out the concentration of locals and who they really are.

The church has been able to identify some of the significant micro-cultures or 'touchpoints' with whom they have sought to make connections—the most significant example being the artistic community. There is a concentration of so-called "creative-types" in the area (perhaps a by-product of the suburb's location in the northern part of NSW's South Coast), plus a number of full-time professional artists within their church community. Since a lot of what their "Hub" space does is cater to groups like local community artists, they have been able to connect with this micro-culture and thus utilize their "Hub" space for art lessons: "They know that we exist, and they know that we let people use that space."

They have also been able to develop some (what the Senior Minister calls) 'soft' community connections that come through groups who use the 'Hub' space; for example for preparing food to be distributed to those in need in the community.

Another example for 'A' Church is obviously with the sporting scene. The Senior Minister has observed that soccer has had more of an external impact upon the church than Surf Life Saving (only about a dozen out of their church population of 320 would have a regular involvement with the Surf Life Saving community). Having said that, his observation was that both sports are a significant part of the lifestyle fabric of this coastal community. Again, a common thrust across the churches in this area is the seasonal tensions: it's not uncommon to see some families very little because of extra-curricular activities.

For 'A' Church, there is a strong focus on building bridges from the community into the church as can be seen from the qualitative findings.

Despite the aspirational nature of the coastal contexts, 'A' Church is working hard to understand and connect with their suburb. The members of 'A' church have even adopted a kind of urban spirituality mentality that walks the streets and prays for the community. The Senior Minister has set the tone for this by spending intentional time with his family at the beach and dog parks where he says they are guaranteed to see the same people almost every day. This is something that will be explored further in Chapter 5.

'P' Church

The Senior Minister of 'P' Church described their church as a welcoming church with a strong willingness to try new things. Historically, this has been seen in fresh thinking when it came to reaching the suburb and, in some cases, showing some risk-taking. There is also a godliness in the way church members live out their faith, stemming from a love for the Scriptures. Both of these factors have led to a strong sense of mission-mindedness.

For various reasons, a number of years ago, 'P' Church amalgamated with a neighbouring parish. While there are advantages in this kind of merger with regard to the ability to combine resources for more effective ministry, there are also the challenges of having congregations across two suburbs which have some significant cultural differences. For example, the Senior Minister observed that the church in the suburb further north was quite protective and fearful of interference—they were happier doing their own thing. The ensuing impact of the merger has seen some people leave. However, those who did leave ended up gathering in smaller home groups (expressing a sense of disenfranchisement with organized church). For around ten years the northern-most church only really had a Sunday morning ministry. The Senior Minister described the culture as a "holy huddle", with the church stuck in maintenance mode rather than being on mission. If anyone was to be invited it was along the lines of come join "our club".

Other challenges are, once again, external sociologically. Common across the board in our findings is that the lifestyle of the suburb competes against church to the extent that the Senior Minister has observed a decrease in members engaging in regular roles in ministry: in his words, "Church sometimes plays second fiddle." Being across two suburbs means each suburb has its own subculture. One challenge in this particular coastal context is at least half of those who own property don't actually live there—there's a significant proliferation of holiday homes. The church feels the impact of the surrounding suburban lifestyle. This has had the tendency to play out in the way parents have a strong influence in what their children are involved in when it comes to extra-curricular activities. Some of these activities are born out of the various community hubs. It is unsurprising that the local SLSC is just one of those, with some church families involved in Nippers. The challenge brought to bear by Nippers, he observes, is that those families involved are either comfortable turning up late to church or are more apathetic and just go straight home after Nippers. They haven't yet found a way to "cater" for that, nor "conquer" it.

The Senior Minister shared the reflections of one church member who felt unhappy with the push of the Surf Club to invest your life in it: "If you sign up for the club you really do sign up for the club". This seems to be a common factor across all Surf Lifesaving Clubs. Interestingly, the tight-knit family bond within the Club has proven difficult to break into. "I don't feel like they need the support back this way or they don't think they need the support . . . they've already got it within the club." There are other micro-cultures of note like the sailing clubs, the RSL and the other (more exclusive) SLSC which are all "ever on his mind". When pressed on what it could look like for mission in the local community to build more of a link to some of these community hubs through chaplaincy, the Senior Minister outlined some of the thinking of the ministry team in terms of how the Assistant Minister could be released into that field. However, the expectations in terms of time have thus far been a roadblock. This raises the question of raising up chaplains from the laity and having them trained in community chaplaincy.

The area, as our findings attest, is again a *destination*. This means it is highly aspirational especially amongst families who move into the area and for those who have retired to the area. The tie-in here is that various community hubs (like the sailing fraternity) are "part of people's vision for how the rest of their life is going to look." This is especially the case for retirees, but perhaps families build their life on that vision too. The Senior Minister explained it in this way: "for many people it is their ideal: 'this is how my life is going to look and I will do what I can to foster and fuel that narrative because this is what I've been dreaming of, this is what I've been planning towards." He pointed to a type of *"carpe diem"* mantra which he has observed which says: "I'm going to give it my all right now, because I know I've got right now and don't know what's going to happen tomorrow". For many in the area, it is the pinnacle of life to live in this area—it is almost their heaven. Therefore, it is not surprising that 'P' Church wants to show people that there is actually something better: they are constantly looking for ways to use the gospel as a way to counter idea of having reached the destination.

Again, when it comes to ministry activities, like many of our Sydney Anglican churches, outreach occurs through youth and children's ministry and SRE Scripture in the local primary and high schools. While there is scope for growth because of their engagement with the local schools, 'P' Church has found the added impact of other churches in the area which have attracted families.

That has not dissuaded them however, and 'P' Church has sought to still engage in local community activities—including, but not limited to connecting with the local schools. In conjunction with school-run market drives, 'P' Church has run a coffee cart at this local school. They also do regular food drives through Anglicare, with the Senior Minister adding: "We do this because we're the local church". Members seem to be more comfortable with an indirect or "gentler" style of evangelism. Historically, there has been a fear of inviting people to evangelistic courses, so this kind of "soft" outreach has been a good way of getting people comfortable with connecting. In the Senior Minister's words: "I think people are very . . . much more easily engaged when it doesn't involve direct evangelism."

In their attempts to understand their local community, 'P' Church spent much of 2019 on a vision and mission strategy for what they might do theologically and practically. As part of their vision process, time was spent with different demographics within the congregation to understand their age and stage of life and how that relates to living in the area. This allowed them to go into 2020 with a clear idea and strategies of what to do. The focus was largely on how the church connects into the community face-to-face, with one goal in the vision to encourage members to involve themselves in at least one local activity or local club, a big priority being the local school.

From their work on vision and strategy 'P' Church has taken the following steps to be more effective as they seek to engage with their communities:

1. They have sought to pool resources. As was mentioned before, in closing down one site due to its limited ability for growing an effective gospel-centred church, they saw the advantage in drawing back to the main centre. Interestingly, this was the right move to make

strategically, given that half the congregation of the shut-down site resided in the vicinity of what is the main church centre.

2. They have taken the decision to focus more closely on the primary school. There's still an encouragement to be involved in community hubs like the SLSC. However, they have over the last four years built a strong relationship with the school, recognising that the reach into the community is wider. While this may not yet have paid off with gospel growth, 'P' Church is probably not as hidden since they have sought to be more involved in the school's market days. Through something as simple as running a coffee cart, the church has looked at a more long-term approach, seeking to build trust by giving the money received from the coffee cart to the school. 'P' Church has become known as the church who supports their school to the point where in 2019, they were invited by the Principal to run the coffee cart for a parent open day. In a letter they wrote to the Principal thanking them for the privilege, the Senior Minister noted they see it as a way of showing the love of God to their local community. This is a great example of what James Davison Hunter calls "being a faithful presence".

It is clear they are a church taking the long-haul approach. The Senior Minister of 'P' Church recognizes that at about the ten-year mark is where they expect to hit their stride: "you're ingrained in the community enough that people recognize you". This shows that longer term tenure allows a deeper connection in both the church and wider community for more effective and sustained ministry and mission.

'M2' Church

It is worth pointing out up-front that when it comes to gospel growth, 'M2' is an outlier as the graphs in Chapter 1 show.

The Rector has served at 'M2' church for 16 years. It has a number of strengths, including its geographical location, with the Rector noting: "You can't understand 'M2' Church without understanding its geographical position." Situated physically in the centre of the village suburb, 'M2' Church is located in a high-profile building and there are a lot of passers-by. This constant foot traffic makes it "one of the most walked past churches in the country . . . 10 million walk past the front door every year." However, many will never actually set foot in the church building. It is not your normal suburban church; in fact, it has all the hallmarks of an urban area, except it is located by the beach. Perhaps that is why it is one of the few family-friendly spaces in the area. The church enjoys a strong "cradle to grave" ministry; it has many able lay people and a strong staff team.

But as with any church, it too faces a number of challenges. It has one of the highest demographic turnovers in the state of NSW. This is partly due to the fact that 85% of housing is in units, apartments, townhouses or semis; 15% stand alone. According to census data it is the exact reverse of the state averages. The high density population (more so than Cronulla) with a concentration of apartments means a higher degree of transition. Also, like other areas we have researched, the larger demographic band is with young single workers. This means that people are often only around for a season and then they move on.

The Rector tells the story of one person living in the area—a single mum with three kids hanging on by their teeth in a tiny little 3-bedroom unit. "They love it but they eventually move," he observes. The Rector re-counted a similar story (not uncommon to these areas with high living costs) about another family with two kids who are moving to Brisbane to purchase a house on a large block of land.

Additionally, a higher felt need of pastoral issues needing to be dealt with is something which comes with urban ministry. There is a higher con-centration of homelessness and mental health issues than one might see in a suburban church, alongside pockets of housing commission families—a classic feature of inner-city living. While characteristically, suburbia is 'settled' with lots of houses and nuclear families typically making up the suburb, with apartments one tends to find more single-parent families. The Rector notes that divorcees end up here for a kind-of sea change.

There's also the significant challenge of affluence: people just don't think they need God. He says:

> Even though you'll have people come with brokenness . . . once the brokenness, although the pain of it goes, they'll—you'll see them disappear. Not all of them. Some of them do come to faith but the affluence absolutely impacts people's openness to the gospel.

Sociologically it was observed that the suburb in which 'M2' Church is located is one of the big destinations for expat workers. It is one of those "high-end postcodes" which again gives it that tribal feel especially since it boasts its own sporting team (like Cronulla). And again like many of the churches in these contexts it is a destination suburb: "people move here because they want to be here. It's like the end of the road, where you settle down (those who are buying anyway)." However one of the marked differences to other suburbs along this stretch is the feature of fewer retirees and more workers. The goal and prize of living here is its proximity to the city.

Another interesting sociological feature for this suburb is its secular culture. Although it's one of the last "Anglo-Saxon enclaves" in the country, the deconstruction of the Christian faith is alive and well with the nations that come into the suburb (a mix of white Anglo-Saxons from European backgrounds along with a smattering of South Africans and Americans). As an example of the secular nature of the suburb (reflecting the wider state of New South Wales), 75% of this electorate voted in favour of same-sex marriage in the 2018 plebiscite. This tells us something about the liberalisation and deconstruction of the Christian worldview which, in the view of the Rector, is strongly tied to an aspirational desire to have an experience-rich life. "They talk about living the dream here. When the surf is up, not as many people are working . . . Don't try and get a tradie (sic) when the surf is pumping."

Although it is seen as a "high-end" postcode, the suburb does not display its wealth as much as other suburbs, but like other suburban or coastal contexts with an urban/suburban mix, one will often find a mix of those at the lower end of the socio-economic spectrum, including housing commission mixing side-by-side with millionaires, "and you won't necessarily be able to pick them because they're both wearing t-shirts, shorts and thongs."

When it comes to the ministry of 'M2' Church and the outreach they want to see happen, we find many of the programs typical of churches. They have two playgroups, typically seeking to reach young families. From this ministry they have seen conversion growth. Through their English as a Second Language (ESL) courses, they run a follow-up group for those who wish to study the Scriptures, out of which has formed a women's Bible study. Through SRE Scripture in local schools, they look to build bridges to youth ministry that's run on Friday nights. Growth in youth has also come via a Kids' Club running on Friday afternoons (their focus is on Years 4-5) in which around half of the children attending are from unchurched families. Overall a third of youth and children are from non-Christian backgrounds (and some of these children have come from Kids' Holiday Clubs as well).

In terms of formal evangelistic outreach, 'M2' Church offers the Alpha course. Over the last few years, they have discovered that courses like

Christianity Explained/Explored or Simply Christianity are less effective with the suburb's demographic. The Rector observes that "Alpha is a course that provides the opportunity for people to have conversations." With a "plug and play" format, one of Alpha's strengths is that it gets people involved; it's not just a monologue (one feature that's different to some of the other courses) which is important because,

> . . . opinionated "Northern Beaches types" want to share. So Alpha provides a journey for people that involves genuine listening . . . Alpha is gospel-like . . . but that's all they can take in. Like, they're so far from the Christian message in so many ways that you just need something that you can start a conversation with . . .

However, an element not particular to Alpha is that most people do not get converted quickly, though it has led to small groups of people forming who will read the Scriptures together. As with any of these kinds of courses, the Rector observed that "it's a long process, so you need to take the long-term view with it and work out how you will keep connected with them."

One of the ways they keep connected with new people is via "newcomers" events which they run every quarter. These are necessary to run since 'M2' Church's Sunday services are the big "front door" as we mentioned before, with a huge number of passers-by. Pre-COVID-19, their open-door ministry allowed them to give away gospel material to those coming in off the street mid-week.

In seeking to engage with and understand their suburb and its culture, 'M2' Church has been able to target some of the significant "touchpoints" within their community. By identifying these, the church has been able to establish a ministry to the fringes, reaching out to the homeless and those struggling with mental health issues. For example, they run a weekly soup kitchen. It's not only those with mental health issues, it is those who are dislocated, or on the edge of society: a ministry of compassion with an evangelistic edge. Those who attend get looked after physically through a meal and even sometimes clothing, but they hear the gospel as well. Each week there is a Bible study as part of the meal. It is one bridge into the church.

This has given 'M2' Church a good reputation in the area. In addition to the soup kitchen, they serve the local primary school. Recognising their proximity to the school and how sometimes even school communities struggle for volunteers to do various jobs around the place, the church deliberately sought to build a relationship by way of offering to do a 'Backyard Blitz' (a working bee) each year as a way of blessing the school. This is a good example of what embracing an urban spirituality and being a faithful presence looks like. They do whatever jobs the school needs done for a day and the church pays for the materials, "because it is a demographic standard for their families".

In order to reach the Surf Life Saving community and Nipper families, 'M2' Church runs a Sunday afternoon service so families involved in Nippers can come at 5pm. The Rector was keen to point out that the prevalence of Nippers was not the only reason for running a 5pm service, since the culture of these suburban coastal contexts means there is a pull towards all sorts of activities. They have structured things in such a way that alongside their Sunday morning church service, there is a kids' program which caters to children up to Year 5. Beyond that, there is the expectation that those children with their families will then "graduate" to the afternoon and go along to 5pm church, where they provide a full high school program. He was quick to point out that younger kids are obviously still welcome at this service as well. This has been very important and has created an effective ministry "flow" in the life of their church. They have some connection with Surf Life Saving chaplaincy through a part-time staff member of their church serving as the Chaplain at a neighbouring Surf Life Saving Club, providing another bridge for families from the Club into the church.

In amongst all this, 'M2' Church, through the leadership of their Rector, has put time into the following areas of church life: he sees discipleship and training people as being of great importance, particularly recognising the value in giving church members the confidence to be promoting the gospel in their "spheres of influence". Alongside this, there has for a number of years been a significant culture of encouragement to bring friends to church.

Prayer is woven into the fabric of church life. 'M2' Church holds weekly prayer meetings, and they begin the year with a week of prayer and fasting. With prayer nights scattered throughout the year, prayer is a significant and visible factor in the life of the church.

Furthermore (in addition to ensuring ministries are run well), the Rector observes that there is no substitute for preaching and teaching and loving people well. He cites the example of McDonald's (Maccas) which always strove for a consistently high level of customer service. "With Maccas", he said, "you know what you're getting," and he has sought to apply that mantra to all their ministries. He points also to a creativity that's important to have in running ministries where you have to keep trying to work out how you do the same thing (important in Anglican ministry) but add something to it to "freshen it up", yet with a message that remains unchanged.

He also points to the importance of hiring good staff, keeping staff, and looking after staff. A staff team with gifted leaders is incredibly important, but they also need to fit the culture of the suburb—both the demographic and ministry culture. He says they don't necessarily need to be a surfer, but they need to understand the surrounding culture and work out how they're going to engage with it.

Aside from the usual seasonal opportunities like Christmas, he sees there's great gospel benefit in seizing opportunities when things happen locally. For many years 'M2' Church has been involved in the suburb's Jazz Festival. One of the great advantages of their location was being able to run a gospel-themed jazz service in conjunction with the Festival. Being located at one of Australia's more famous beaches, the Australian Open of Surf competition brought with it unique opportunities. In the end, there's great gospel benefit found in harnessing the connection points mentioned above, but also, keeping on opening the doors to be known amongst the community and build from there:

> It's amazing how many people say, 'Oh yeah, I've walked past you or I've heard the music'. You know? And something sparks in them to go, 'actually I should find out more'. So we're a church of many open doors.

'H' Church

'H' Church is located in a suburb which could be best described as a village. The church itself has grown numerically and fluctuates around the 150-attendance mark. In the 16 years the Senior Minister has been there, they have seen natural attrition with growth in a slightly overall younger mix. Ministry occurs across the age ranges. As with many of these beachside suburbs, the area itself has seen a growth in boutique shops and cafés and an increase in the range of cosmopolitan restaurants. As older folk have died or moved to retirement accommodation, their houses built in the 1940s or 50s have been knocked down and rebuilt by professional couples. The suburb (similar to Cronulla) was once a working-class area socioeconomically but has seen a shift to being more middle-class with working professionals. Again, similar to other pockets of the Northern Beaches, it is still quite an "Anglo enclave", though it has experienced significant growth with an influx of people from the United Kingdom and some South Africans. An influx of young professionals with kids has seen a significant growth in the local schools.

The question again is, how well does 'H' Church reflect the demography of the suburb? 'H' Church is generally well represented across most groups, though under-represented in teenagers alongside people in their 20s. Again this (which we've observed is a common factor) comes down to the proportion of unit-dwellers in their catchment. The suburb just to the south has many units and the church struggles to reach unit-dwellers. Many people rent because of the high cost of housing.

The church community is welcoming and has good contact with outsiders. 'H' Church's vision to share the gospel with their suburb and to see people encounter, believe and grow in Jesus drives much of what they do—especially when it comes to providing what the Senior Minister calls "encounter moments". However, as with many churches, the challenge is found in just getting people to come and encounter Jesus. In considering when the last time was that they had a newcomer walk through their doors, he said, " . . . they're not even experiencing it in the first place to reject it . . . " This is due to a couple of factors. One is that for many in the suburb (and this is common in our findings across suburban coastal contexts), the suburb is "heaven"; that is, it's the ultimate place to live and there's not much better. "Therefore, why would they think they need Jesus?"

Further, because people are generally quite self-sufficient (there isn't a high social need), creating those opportunities with them to give Jesus some consideration is a challenge.

The high prevalence of leisure opportunity with an easily-accessible beach, children's sport (Sunday is now the day given to that); the local Surf Life Saving Club and Nippers, give the feeling of irrelevance; the church is largely forgotten because the suburb is such a good place to live. The Senior Minister described it to us as a lot of "worshipping the creation rather than the creator."

> When you go to the beach you really can find another alternative satisfying spirituality . . . at the beach you can really feel like you get away from some of your troubles and feel a sense of other.

There's a disconnection available from the grind of life. So instead of the God of the Bible, people settle for the physical, but attribute a form of spirituality to it—so there really is a liturgy attached to the beach and the associated lifestyles.

Amongst the myriad of extra-curricular activities we find within these suburban coastal contexts is the common thread of Nippers. 'H' Church has only a handful of families involved. (It is just an accepted part of being a church in this context that Nippers will impact upon them). The impact of Nippers at this 'H' Church means, for example, that one family will head to another church close by across the summer months since that church has a 5pm gathering.

In a similar vein to another church that was interviewed, families will attempt the Nippers/church combination and end up arriving late to church. However, this can often wear thin after some time, since there is more effort involved (children will be fairly tired after a morning of Nippers and if the weather is inclement, then they'll more than likely just go home).

For three years, 'H' Church ran a "beach church" initiative with the help of one of their ministers at the time (who later was invited to be the Chaplain to the local SLSC). The focus was on having a post-Nippers church service next to the Surf Club, under a tent. Though this was discontinued mainly because of a lack of gospel growth or "fruit" and low attendance, it's worth pointing out that those involved in running it grew in their evangelistic and ministry/mission-mindedness. Good "fruit" for the team evolved, but at the end of the day, there wasn't a lot of gospel growth to show for it. This highlights a strategic problem for all churches in their attempts to engage with the Nippers community: most families are content to just head home after Nippers. Interestingly, the Senior Minister pointed out that it was hard for them to move their contacts from a simple lightweight service under a tent to a church service, even if it might be family friendly and contemporary. This highlights for us the issue of trying to take church out of its setting and to some extent the issue of the incarnational model of ministry. It also highlights an issue of building up the Christians and carrying around the expectation of rolling out a whole church.

One interesting observation made by the Senior Minister is that Nippers aren't winning the battle when it comes to Sunday morning commitment either. The whole process requires an army of volunteers and sometimes the attendance among the less-committed is even less than regular church attendance. (Not all are local, with many coming from the North Shore suburbs—about a half hour drive). Further, he pointed out that if kids don't like it they're not forced to keep doing it and there is a higher drop-out rate than you might imagine.[11]

Most of the ministries/activities of 'H' Church would be deemed attractional. Alongside the regular youth and children's ministries are "one-to-one" Bible reading amongst congregation members, follow-up of newcomers, and a Holiday Kids' Club, mainly held on pupil-free days. The church seeks to reach out through initiatives like a Seniors' lunch once a month with a speaker (not often Christian) and doorknocking in the suburb, along with letterbox drops of postcards advertising special events. Prior to COVID-19, they ran a market day whenever there was a fifth Saturday in the month.

As a way of making inroads into the lifestyle-driven nature of the suburb, the Assistant Minister was looking to begin a "fitness boot camp" over a period of 4 weeks. The thinking behind it was to encourage church members in their 20s and 30s to invite their friends along to a session in a local park with a meal afterwards. The struggle is working out how to turn this pre-evangelistic initiative into an "encounter experience" (defined by the Senior Minister as an activity where a person actually hears something of Jesus in some way). At this point, therefore, it is about building and cultivating those relationships. 'H' Church was also exploring the possibility of hosting an Alpha-style evangelistic course off-site (at one of the local clubs). The idea is to utilize other spaces for courses explaining Christianity to give people that 'encounter experience', since they're not coming through the doors of the church.

In their desire to understand their community through studying the National Church Life Survey data, 'H' Church identified points of vulnerability or "touchpoints" within the community. The church ran a seminar entitled "Raising Kids" and invited a psychologist to speak about anxiety and depression in children. Of the 45 who attended, around 30 had no previous connection with the church. While these steps haven't brought them to the point of encountering Jesus, it is nonetheless a step. These are

---

11. The writer's observation from a combination of the qualitative research and his years of involvement in Surf Life Saving both as a volunteer lifesaver and chaplain attests to this drop-out rate once 'Nippers' reach a certain age. The challenge for Surf Life Saving Clubs like churches is to work out how they can improve at those major age-transition points. This is a point that our interview with the former President of one Surf Life Saving Club confirms.

all little steps towards people meeting Jesus, which takes time. However, effort needs to be taken to look at the next "bridge" or "step" for people to able to do that and to build upon those connections. In order to facilitate this, 'H' Church has a goal that 20% of non-church families who come to a Kids' Holiday Club will come to a Sunday service. Hosting a Sunday Funday on the Sunday straight after the pupil free day inviting families to come along to church gave them contact with a couple of families who wouldn't have otherwise set foot in church.

A tangible result from the planted "beach church" was one of the staff team being invited to be the Chaplain at the SLSC. For various reasons, he left to join the staff team at a neighbouring church. Because this church had an afternoon service it gave him the opportunity to invite "contacts" from the Surf Club to church on Sunday afternoons.

It is worth noting that through the Chaplain's ministry, one of 'H' Church's (and SLSC) members has done a Sports Chaplaincy course. She has subsequently been recognized with her accreditation as an Assistant Chaplain at that Surf Club.

This has given her good opportunities to show care and even share her faith. The "soft" impact that comes through Life Saving Chaplaincy shows us the indirect gospel impact that the chaplaincy model can achieve through this ministry of presence. It also matches up with the minister's refrain that "we want the chance that someone might get to encounter Jesus".

In the end, this is God's Spirit working to change people's hearts and minds. The church is the instrument or the vehicle through which that can occur. So our research shows that many, if not all of the churches interviewed, are working hard at leveraging existing connections they have in current ministries but also harnessing other cultural touchpoints. The Senior Minister pointed to Halloween as another example of a 'touchpoint' that they were looking at, to try to use this as a way of connecting with families.

'M1' Church

'M1' Church is located in Sydney's Eastern Suburbs. Due to its proximity to a large university and hospital (plus other large employers), the congregation has enjoyed the benefit of people who were trained in university student ministry and therefore value solid Bible teaching. The Rector describes the church as eclectic, in that it enjoys difference and a crossover of cultures. Geographically, the Rector describes it as perhaps the third best site within the suburb where you would hope to have a church. The church has a solid staff team, plus a few core members who form the "backbone" of the church. He sees them as a flexible church.

Like the other churches we interviewed, there's the challenge surrounding the rising cost of living and other costs due to the nature of the area. Though this, as the Rector pointed out, has pluses and minuses attached to it, there are high net worth individuals who are a great asset in the sense of gospel partnership. However, their high professionalism can pose a threat in an individualistic way: an overly process-driven approach, coupled with that critical core, can sometimes make it difficult to envision them (i.e., get them on board with church direction). Another challenge they have has a church, which is common to these contexts, is the highly transient nature of the suburb with a high percentage of unit/apartment dwellers. This makes connecting with the community a challenge. Additionally, the eclectic nature of the suburb makes it difficult to define the mission and even to choose strategies. Certainly, the cultural climate of the area with a post-Christian society coupled with an apathy towards religion make ministry and mission harder in this context. Like many of the other suburbs, a common demographical aspect sees an above national average of 20-40-year-olds living in the area. There is a high concentration of units of high-density makeup as well as a high turnover in accommodation. Again, it is one of those "destination suburbs" with, in the Rector's words, "people who are here for a good time not a long time."

In a similar fashion to the other ministers who were interviewed, a good understanding of the NCLS data has helped the staff team to shape a tailored approach to mission in a strong way. For seven years, that Census insight shaped them towards being an eclectic boutique church (matching the suburb), rather than perhaps a semi-urban church which would probably reflect the data more closely. The Rector classifies the area as a "semi-urban suburban coastal city village . . . Which just spells out how hard it is to work out what you should be doing".

Interestingly, his approach from the first seven years has changed, such that he leads the church more like a suburban church "but muting those excesses to keep its eclecticism up."

The demographics upon which he focused early on in his incumbency were in the 20-40 age bracket. From there, this formed the backbone of a church plant in the surrounding area comprising high-rise apartments. It failed for a number of reasons, least of which being they didn't have a strong core team which is needed for a plant to get off the ground. The Rector cites another reason for the failure: " . . . we tried to turn our ecclesiology into evangelism." That is, he tended to look at their programmatic mode of doing church and then attempted to take that out to people in the form of a church plant which, in his words, is "like carrying a church around on your back to reach people". This was touched upon in Chapter 4 in the discussion surrounding the definition and nature of church. The Rector pointed out that the focus of church is people being built in the faith in order to be sent out. People do come to faith in a church setting, but only so many.

He observes importantly that people are having way more encounters outside of church with non-Christian contacts, but there is a sluggishness when it comes to inviting people to church. Perhaps that is why over the years there was a tendency to think in terms of events—what people can invite their friends along to (guest services, evangelistic events or some other program). There is certainly a place for those within the life of the church but, as Chapter 2 showed, our climate has changed in many respects. What 'M1' Church realised and needed to move towards was not programs as such, but a discipleship/people model of ministry. The publication of *The Trellis and the Vine* helps immensely with this much-needed ministry shift in thinking. It can be difficult to swing people's mindset from running events to a more discipleship focus. And while churches shouldn't think of dispensing with events altogether, the all-too-frequent problem is the tendency to see those in the calendar within the life of the church and say, "that's what we do."

It's within this tension, however, that we want to see churches in these contexts building upon their pre-existing relationships and understanding the culture of the area enough for the church to be able to craft and communicate a vision for that area. Thus, the Rector was keen for his people to survey the scene and respond to what opportunities were there. So rather than coming up with a plan, he sees the merit of being responsive to current opportunities within one's context. It can be as simple as inviting a couple of friends who have shown some interest in Christian things to have dinner and coupling that with a Christianity/Life Explored-type course. He says:

> You've just got to work out what the opportunity is and do the most helpful thing for that opportunity . . . I'd rather think about the evangelistic stuff that we have as a bunch of resources on our

shelf . . . outreach is really a few people praying, looking for opportunity and going, okay, what do we take off the shelf.

He drew a diagram which is reproduced below that plots where we do most of our evangelism in our churches:

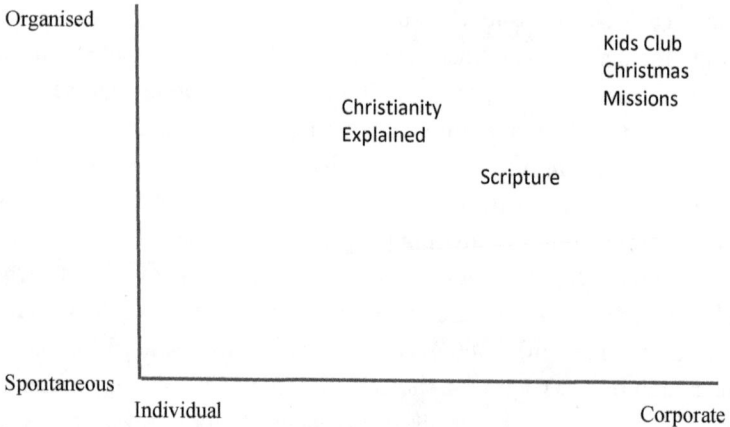

Organised

                                                          Kids Club
                                                            Christmas

                      Christianity   Missions
                      Explained

                                Scripture

Spontaneous

Individual   Corporate

Figure 1: An Example of Evangelism in our Local Churches.

He believes that churches need to try to shift away from the corporate and the organized to more of the individual with a mix of organised and spontaneous. An alternate approach like this takes time, with vision setting, planning, education and training, and communication. It means painting the picture of what you hope to achieve, crafting the vision and then teaching it to a small group of people (like an outreach team for example), who will be able to approach members of the congregation and say, "here's an opportunity—would this be a good thing for us to invite someone along to"? For example, one approach could be to mobilize small groups to help them see themselves as "gospel communities". You could train the small group leaders to provide opportunities for their group to invite friends to a small dinner where relationships are developed and in turn provide further gospel opportunities.

The Rector cited an example of a non-Christian filmmaker who goes along to their church. They had the opportunity to view one of her documentaries, interview her and explore some of the aspects of her work, connecting it to a Christian worldview. There are many other opportunities that can be derived from the things happening within the suburban context that allow for evangelism to take place.

Again, like others in our research, 'M1' Church is currently engaged in everyday ministries (SRE Scripture, youth ministry, etc.). Interestingly, while it may not look like outreach on the surface, the Rector points out that the last ten new youth who joined their youth group were all unchurched. They run a "Guest Service" (with a public gospel explanation) once a term. This is a low-traction opportunity for the gospel with the idea of opening up the conversation around the reason for God (similar to 'H' Church in their desire to provide opportunities for people to have that experience of encountering Jesus). They also run a Kids' Holiday Club (once a year) and like other church leaders I spoke to (from 'H' Church & 'N' Church), an "alternative to Halloween" event. This is important because it recognizes the rising attraction in our culture of Halloween and instead of decrying it, this approach seeks to show that Christianity can actually speak into an event that has more recently become part of the Australian cultural landscape. They also harness the lead-up to Christmas by running a week-long mission partnering with a team of university students.[12]

Overall, 'M1' Church would say they do well with what the Rector calls the "light reach" approach. It is interesting to see how little the regular members sometimes know of their own suburb. This Rector when he arrived, asked members to take him around and show him their suburb, but he discovered that they were fairly disconnected from their area, unengaged in their community and they were unable to show him the real suburb. This points to a concern that we ought to have about our members. Not all the churches experienced the same thing, and the reality is that in areas like these coastal contexts, not everyone in the church will live in the immediate surrounds for reasons that might include affordability, moving church, and even family size, given the high concentration of apartments/units.

The Rector believes (as per the diagram above) that there is much to be gained from encouraging the "individual and spontaneous". This can be as simple as sitting somewhere in the suburb and just observing or speaking to people like local "gatekeepers"—in this case Real Estate Agents, GPs,

---

12. This mission, known around Australia as a National Training Event (NTE) mission is run in conjunction with a number of Christian university groups who are affiliated with the Australian Fellowship of Evangelical Students. The NTE mission is a way of students being able to put into practice skills acquired throughout that week of training in mission and evangelism.

local business owners (the kind of people who understand community) and hearing their stories and cultural observations.

Another factor which the Rector cites is the demands on people's time—there is little room for this kind of community engagement with work, family commitments and then of course church. He points to the issue of churches being over-programmed historically with little time available for people to be released into the community.

'M1' Church has no members involved in Nippers (though they do have some club members at the local SLSC). Other than that, no real attempts have been made to reach the Surf Life Saving community, mainly because early experiments did not generate huge success, plus there was, in the Rector's words, "insufficient native strength." While the Rector finds the idea of reaching the SLS community enormously attractive, he believes he would have found it difficult to take people with him.

Interestingly, the culture of this suburb's beach can be somewhat repelling for people. People are slightly averse to it—they love living in the suburb and the beach has obvious attractive elements, but there are cultural aspects which are somewhat hard to swallow. For example, there's the perception that you have to be a great surfer—"it's not a mum and dad beach."[13] Interestingly, the people who are keen about the beach in their church are surfers, not 'clubbies' (members of the SLSC).

Neither of the two SLS Clubs have a Chaplain associated with them and the Rector wasn't so sure that he as the Rector of the church should automatically be the Chaplain. He did however recognize that a chaplain connected to the local church is a good thing all the same, and this would have gospel implications.

Some of the other initiatives 'M1' Church has explored when it comes to the surrounding micro-cultures included a desire to reach people living in the housing commission area in the South of the suburb, but there seems to be some mental hurdle that needs to be overcome when doing ministry like this in your own area. He pointed out it seems almost easier for people to embrace the idea of going overseas to do the same kind of mission that you could be doing in your own backyard.

Ultimately, the Rector recognizes that it's an enormously complicated area with a coming-together (a clash, almost) of differing micro-cultures. He describes it in this way:

---

13. This beach, in particular, has had a recently chequered history of territorial surfers.

... there are multiple micro-cultures . . . , so the two [SLS] clubs are each different micro-cultures, two surf lifesaving cultures and then we've got three Board Riders Clubs, each a different micro-culture and then within general board riders there are other micro-cultures. Then there's The Housing Commission micro-cultures and there's two of them and they're separated in various ways and then there's school, kind of, private and public and those are stratified in various ways and then there's just a stack of other micro-cultures . . . that are small and fragmentary.

He feels that, with the growth they have had, albeit slowly, they are on the cusp of some good things around the corner, but it's just breaking through that next growth barrier.[14] He acknowledges constraints which he calls "invisible walls", but then there are other constraints that he thinks cause their size to remain exactly where they are: "Anglican buildings are unhelpful".

For 'M1' Church the right strategic decision at the moment is to focus on families with kids. As the Rector says, "the strategic decision is to strengthen your spine"; that is, look at what resources and personnel you have and then what is going on in your area. The people in the case of 'M1' Church who are the "spine of the place" are the locals—the ones who don't move after a few years. Focusing on them and helping them to connect brings an intergenerational longevity. The Rector wants them to continually know how important they are to the growth and effective ministry of the church.

While still captured by the eclectic and the boutique, the Rector can see that the smart and strategic thing is to ensure that ministry is strengthened in such a way that sees church members branching out to other areas and spheres. This means focusing on those you have and equipping them for mission and ministry so they may ultimately permeate the surrounding micro-cultures with the good news of Jesus.

14. There are all sorts of factors that can impede particular growth barriers. For a good treatment of how churches can set themselves up for the impact of breaking through certain growth barriers, refer to Gary L. Mcintosh *Taking Your Church to the Next Level: What Got You Here Won't Get You There* and for a more localised treatment, Gupta, R. 2016. "Why do Sydney Anglican Churches Struggle to Grow Beyond 200?" Dmin thesis, Trinity International University.

'W' Church

The Senior Minister came to a church that had been in plateau for some time and as such he was invited by the Bishop to revitalize the ministry there. He took over a parish that had two buildings in the one suburb: one in close proximity to the beach, the other up the hill nestled in amongst high-density dwellings.

It was clear from the outset that there were particular issues that needed to be addressed including a "siege mentality", which is intriguing as historically there were positive attempts made to connect with the surrounding culture.

In the Senior Minister's first few years in the role, 'W' Church employed an Assistant Minster to "replant" the church across from the beach—basically closing down the ministry there and combining it with what was already established at the site further up the hill. This site up the hill had its challenges; parking and proximity being two major issues.

The opportunity to then merge with a neighbouring parish in 2018 provided them with the solution to some of those issues and the ability to focus more on what was happening at the beach site.

In the last two years, 'W' Church has grown from 28 to 110 parishioners with the growth comprising a mix of new converts and also people with some church background. Within that mix are a number of migrants who moved to Australia and were converted through the Alpha course (this is the biggest traction they have had) or because they had some form of interaction with a congregation member.

Like a number of the churches in these areas with a high cost of living, it has a transient population and thus not a high concentration of kids or youth. Having said that, they have had good traction in terms of outreach through their playgroup ministry—"Hop & Bop" which attracts about 140 (children and parents). It's an outreach program with a music focus and a Bible talk. The Senior Minister describes it as an "engine room for growth", as some have transitioned to church via Alpha. Incidentally Alpha is also an area of outreach focus which has been quite successful.

Early on in his tenure, the Senior Minster spent time surveying the culture, asking: "What is the gospel to the average person living in the area?" The gospel according to this suburb was "living a good life . . . a healthy life, relaxed." There is an anti-institutional attitude amongst people in this suburb, but not anti-spiritual. This was one reason for closing the church at the beach, which had a very formal club-like feel to it with a strong Anglican liturgical bent. Upon closing it and having employed an Associate Minister, they began from scratch to work out how best to reach this particular section of the suburb right next to the beach, realising their focus was going to be on people in the 25-39 age bracket, some of whom, they knew from research, lived in de-facto relationships but who valued community, and who did not tend to drive. Aiming towards reaching them meant recognising that the now-merged congregation up the hill was reaching a different area and demographic.

Despite the high cost of living, there is still a high concentration of families, and culturally, family is valued. This is seen in the uptake of families coming to the playgroup ministry. As such, the church has settled on this as a 'touchpoint', running parenting courses, marriage courses, and courses focusing on anxiety and mental health. Some of these have been run in partnership with Anglicare.

With the added realisation that people gather in communities, 'W' Church has a sustained focus on community hubs. With a strong Surf Life Saving culture associated with the suburb, the Associate Minister and some other congregation members joined the local Surf Life Saving Club. It has enabled the Associate Minister to share some chaplaincy duties with another local church member. The involvement of two of their elders as members of the Club has sometimes led to a proportion of people from church attending social events at the Club which "has a bit of an impact on the tone, if nothing else."

Because locals love the beach, and people "love doing whatever they can to be a part of the beach," 'W' Church in this vicinity of the beach went through a strategic planning process, establishing a mission and vision, and as a result has seen some significant and positive growth. In the Senior Minister's words, "they've got a healthy view about what the mission looks like, what evangelism looks like, what effective evangelism looks like". They identified a need to focus on the "true locals": long-term residents, shorter-term "creatives" and high-flying business-types including those involved in the TV/film industry. Thus, their mission model has been to connect through the local cafés, schools (via SRE Scripture) as well as local community groups (such as Surf Life Saving) and the local council.

With a congregation of around 60 at the beach site, one third of those are active members of the SLSC. They have established that faithful Christian presence which was explored in the previous chapter. The Senior Minister cites one example of a lady from their church who is:

. . . a member of the Girls on Boards . . . And she prays for what we're doing with the church and has been very positive about the impact she's seen . . . there's a few board clubs that our church members are part of . . . [and] see it as part of what they do in being Christians.

'W' Church also made the decision in its revitalisation phase to not do morning church because of the clash with Nippers on a Sunday morning. Recognising the strong impact historically that an institution like Nippers has on the community led them to structure the timing of a new church gathering around Nippers. Many of the children who attend SRE Scripture classes at the local public school attend Nippers. With their Assistant Minister teaching SRE Scripture and also involved at the Club, this has provided them with inroads to establish relationships.

The church has recognized the futility of trying to compete with Nippers and so are continuing to explore other options (e.g., Saturday nights or even mid-week), that might be more effective when it comes to church timing to really connect well with these families.

'W' Church also has a solid discipleship strategy across the whole church which they call "DNA groups", similar to mid-week Bible study or "growth groups". Made up of a small number (3-4 people), they have deliberately set a lower bar, recognising the busyness of urban Sydney people. While some would point to this and say they're encouraging mediocrity in people's Christian walk, the Senior Minister was at pains to point out that this discipleship model is particularly applied to those Nipper families. Again, facilitated by the Assistant Minister, it's a way of encouraging people in their walk with Jesus on a regular basis but not placing so much of a burden upon them. The groups, interestingly, have grown and have become part of the culture of the church and something that people look forward to. They are "the key ways of pastoring" and ensuring people are well cared for.

In the Senior Minister's words: "the . . . church has a positive coagulating effect since one of the yearnings of the people who live in the area is for community."

The ministry team has worked hard at researching what people's longings are and how the gospel can speak to those longings: so, for example, where people would describe their longing for nature as getting into the outdoors and enjoying that healthy lifestyle, the church reframes it as a way of helping them "to make connections between what their hearts really long for—that sense of community and belonging."

There is this strong desire to enjoy the benefits of the locale where they work (Sydney CBD) and the money and a stable job which go with that, coupled with the benefits of beauty and nature that come with living next to the beach. This is what an urban coastal context provides. 'W' Church, therefore, is seeking to show how people's hopes and longings can be answered by the Christian worldview.

This is a great example of what Tim Keller's contextualisation looks like in practice. That is, helping people resonate with the church and saying that your longings aren't wrong things per se—they are actually good, but you are looking in the wrong place to find satisfaction in those things. The gospel actually speaks deeply into those longings, which allows people to come to a right understanding so that they can worship the Creator who provides these good things for them to enjoy. The nexus between spiritual and mental health is also a good example of this as the church attempts to allow the gospel to speak into this point of vulnerability for many people, which sees them turning to the lifestyle and trappings of the beach to keep mentally healthy. As we explore some potential ways forward in the next chapter, unpacking the secular liturgy of the beachside context will be important.

'C' Church

The Rector of 'C' church has been in the role for a little over two decades. He arrived straight from Bible College as the Assistant Minister and later transitioned into the role of Rector. 'C' Church is located in a suburban coastal context. While they were once strong in kids' and youth ministries, these have dissipated. Like many churches, their heyday was in the 70s and 80s when they enjoyed strong ministries across a large demographic range.

The struggles and the challenges they face in their coastal context have meant a narrow focus on a few things, such as a pre-school, that is part of the local church. Before COVID-19 threw many programs into disarray, there was a focus on running Simply Christianity with the staff and parents of the children.

The population demography, not uncommon to these suburban coastal contexts, sees a huge spike in the 25-40 age bracket, coupled with the prevalence of apartments or units because it is one of the premier beach suburbs. Again, it is a "destination" suburb, considered "the place to be". The bars, restaurants, entertainment and lifestyle all attract people who are thinking about everything other than Jesus. The issue for 'C' Church, again not uncommon, is their disconnect between the make-up of the church and the demographic of the suburb, with an average age of 57 amongst their members.

The main challenge to any kind of ministry to children/families comes in the form (again) of local Nippers with a registration at the Surf Club close to 1000. The church leverages off a pre-school establishment they have control over which operates as a Christian pre-school. Some pastoral contacts flow into the church as they might from the local Anglican school and public school.

A significant exodus of staff from the church, both paid and unpaid, over the previous 12 months has left the church in an interesting position. The church is hoping to employ someone who will connect and engage with the pre-school on a part-time basis—getting to know the parents and kids with a view to intentionally building that bridge between the pre-school and church.

As with the other churches whose Senior Ministers we interviewed, there is a strong focus on SRE Scripture as a vehicle for engagement and a channel for advertising various church-based initiatives.

'C' Church also continues to be involved in some of the traditional and distinctive parish-based actives like ANZAC ceremonies. It is events like ANZAC Day which tap into that modern spirituality. There's a secular liturgy attached to ANZAC Day and especially the ceremony. In the words of the Rector:

> It helps you (a) speak about the meaning of sacrifice in front of an audience who wouldn't normally give much thought to this kind of thing and (b) it puts you in front of local dignitaries whom I now have a good relationship with.

In the early days of the Rector's ministry, 'C' Church poured energy into a lot of letterbox drops and advertising in the local paper.

As a way of equipping their people to get talking about Jesus, 'C' Church conducts an evangelistic training course entitled *Just Start Talking*, with the aim that this will flow onto bigger attendances. While this particular kind of course-based ministry initiative doesn't target any particular group per se, the reason for trying a course like *Just Start Talking* is to get that mode of conversation back on the agenda in the minds of people at church and to energize and equip them to be ready to have a conversation and even look for ways to put little "gospel bytes" into the everyday.

The demographic make-up of the suburb sees people of predominantly Roman Catholic background (that being the box ticked on the Census form). Interestingly, attendance at the Catholic Church is ten times that of the Anglican church. While there are many distractions within a "destination" suburb with a strong lifestyle focus like this one, families seem to be more open to Christian things which means the church is freer to run an overtly Christian playgroup. And although at the time of interview the playgroup was closed because of COVID-19, the Rector notes that families are still more open to Christian "things" than the young singles or couples without kids.

In their attempts to connect with the suburb, 'C' Church has focused on attractional ministry. An evening service was started in 2009 to try to reach the younger demographic and for a while they had an Assistant Minister who was himself in that demographic, but he moved on. Unfortunately, they haven't seen as much success as they would have expected with that evening service.

'C' Church has a couple of families involved in the local Surf Life Saving Club. When asked how they go about encouraging families involved to still gather intentionally, given that the season runs over almost half the year now, a couple of examples were proffered to highlight the difficulties they face. The Rector said:

> . . . one of the families, [a] mum we came into contact [with] through playgroup, two daughters, dad doesn't believe, okay, so the daughters they started here just as one or two year olds and now they are in Year two and Year six, something like that but the mum will come to church and say well, dad's taken the kids to Nippers. I mean, what can you say? Tell your husband he's an idiot and then another example from a few years back was just extraordinary. A family, mum, dad and the two kids came and when the younger child got to Nippers age the mother said to us one day well, we won't be coming anymore, or the kids won't be coming because God has told me that it's better to take the kids to Nippers than church. I mean, it's something you don't even engage with because it's so out there. That's the power . . .

That pull shows what churches in these coastal contexts face, whether it's Nippers or other sports. But perhaps instead of saying, 'Well we tried 'X' to attract people to us and it worked for a while', or even expecting families where one spouse (more often than not the husband) isn't a Christian to just turn up, (which can sometimes make it very difficult to sway things), perhaps there needs to be a more intentional focus on discipleship and a preaching that captures people's hearts. He put it this way:

> . . . what is it that needs to happen? The only answer that I can give to that is they've got to have an experience of faith. They've got to have some Holy Spirit experience or some profound experience which will cause them to say Jesus is king. Not just intellectually but by heart.

'N' Church

'N' Church is a Baptist church in a coastal suburb in Sydney. The Senior Pastor has been employed at the church for nearly 20 years. The church has enjoyed a strong Bible teaching heritage with a strong focus on preaching and small group ministry. This has meant a desire to see church members equipped to be able to handle the Scriptures confidently. An outworking of this, as people have been equipped biblically and theologically, is that they have also been mobilized for mission and engagement in the local area.

Historically, 30 years ago 'N' Church may have adopted what the Senior Pastor calls a "fortress mentality". And although that brought with it the potential to not be as engaged with local community at that time, they still "really wanted to hold fast to what it meant to trust God in his word."

Despite being located in a highly transient area, 'N' Church also has a solid history of being able to retain faithful people. With a highly mobile younger population, they enjoy good relational connections. In fact, the last decade saw significant conversion growth amongst families who themselves became passionate about evangelism. Their vibrant faith drew others in, and they saw "quite an astonishing growth in that ministry area." He described the church as "a really generous and vital church."

Because of its strong music ministry, it has for some time attracted those musical and creative types.

The church has also intentionally fostered an intergenerational culture. Even when other churches were moving towards and embracing the model of the Homogeneous Unit Principle,

'N' church sought to have multiple generations; older and younger people mixing together at church across their morning and evening gatherings.

Like all of the churches whose ministers were interviewed, 'N' Church faces the challenge of being located in an area where people say, "This is kind of heaven on earth, and so why would I need anything beyond that?" With a high value placed on weekend recreation because many people travel a distance to get to work in the Sydney CBD, there's a huge focus on exercise, recreation and lifestyle across the weekend, but notably on Sundays, since Saturdays are given over to sport. This was one of the hypotheses that the writer sought to confirm from the experience of his own area.

The desire for a feeling of security makes engaging evangelistically a challenge, but, as the Senior Pastor pointed out, in this affluent area with high property prices, it pushes the younger generations away. He described it in this way:

> . . . that movement of people who potentially grow up and fami-
> lies that grew up through the church, there's a high percentage . . .
> that end up having to move into either other areas of Sydney or
> out of [the] State . . . And so you're regularly farewelling people
> who are being equipped and dispersed and sent, which is a good
> thing but also a sad thing.

Coupled with this are other cultural emphases common to these contexts, including a high emphasis on education and the opportunities given to kids. The Senior Pastor has observed a real emphasis on parents providing the best for their children across many areas. It's this extra-curricular focus which "floods in" from outside the church to parents in the church and, he points out, is often played against the value of the youth group or other discipleship activities.

Some other struggles they face are certainly felt across all churches, including working out what it means to be the church in a changing culture, and then the struggles around relational issues intertwined with church unity and discipline. There has been the challenge also of how they constitute themselves which is peculiar to their denominational tradition.

One of their big strategic emphases for some years now has been thinking about what it means to be deployed in mission and equipping people for this. With one of their core strengths being a twin focus around evangelism and discipleship, people are deployed both in a formal and informal sense. This sees people encouraged to involve themselves in programs ranging from larger events and work in prisons to community groups; but then also thinking missionally in terms of their own families and workplaces. They see their school SRE Scripture, and midweek children's and youth ministry programs as part of that formal approach to outreach.

Tied in with this, 'N' Church has a strong heritage of mission and a history of supporting link missionaries overseas. Because members are able to grasp hold of what mission means, they have a strong 'sending" culture. A shift in recent years to the '5Ms' ministry model[15] meant they have been able to keep mission clearly on the agenda with a constant refrain around the theme of what it looks like to be called and sent. The Senior Pastor described their "slogan" as them being "a family on mission, making disciples of Jesus Christ". This has been significant for them in their impact on their community, because "participation in that mission has been very intentional and a significant focus [which they] taught and preached around." Therefore, they're constantly asking and getting people to articulate what it looks like for *them* to be on mission in their street or their neighbourhood, workplace or family. The fruit of a significant missional focus such as this one has been that people recognize those opportunities and the church has been able to train and equip them for that task.

Again, as with most of the churches that were interviewed, 'N' Church's ministry team has worked hard with Census data (both NCLS and other sociological research) to understand their suburban demography and movements. This has enabled them to "embark on various different kinds of strategic plans." Interacting with the data has allowed them to understand their community, target particular spaces and ask what's happening culturally and philosophically around them, in an effort to understand and engage with some of the different micro-cultures. It has also pushed them to create environments where people feel comfortable to invite their friends into certain kinds of spaces (e.g., harnessing music since there's a strong culture within that space, and an emphasis around men's and women's events). However, due to church members' poor follow-up after these events, they've shifted their focus to a local beach

---

15. The 5 'Ms' Model of ministry is a shift from the more traditional structure where a team of ministers might be responsible for a particular congregation (i.e. morning or evening) to a structure where each minister/pastor has oversight for a specific area of church life. The name of the model is taken from Rick Warren's *Purpose Driven Church* in which he outlines five specific purposes that he believes God wants every church to pursue. These areas/portfolios are: Maturity; Membership; Magnification; Ministry and Mission.

mission—along similar lines to 'A' Church. In this ministry/outreach focus, they planted both a young adults' and kids' mission in the same vein as one would find with a Scripture Union Beach Mission. These have been "incredibly helpful community engagement places" because they've been able to connect locally in a different way.

In talking about connections, when asked about the impact of the Surf Life Saving communities and how the church has sought to connect with this micro-culture (among others), the Senior Pastor pointed out that it's not Surf Life Saving per se that takes people away from the Sunday gathering, but rather Nippers. 'N' Church investigated restructuring their morning services, wondering if a later timeslot would allow those who were involved in Nippers to come to church afterwards. Initial enthusiasm with the idea never really translated into anything concrete.

He is of the opinion that the way a church can minister to the Surf Club is "by being a clubbie and being involved in those groups." They have a number of church members on patrol as Surf Life Savers regularly through the summer and therefore are relationally engaged in that space. Interestingly, the Senior Pastor observed that over winter, the local Rugby League team, when playing their home games on Sundays, have more of an impact on Sunday evening, with lower congregational attendance.

The Senior Pastor is working hard at giving church members a framework for being able to speak the gospel well into the lives of those around them. He does this by helping them to understand how people think and how the gospel speaks into that and why they can have a confident trust and hope in Jesus whatever the scenarios or situations that might come across their paths. He acknowledges that this kind of training and discipleship is slower to roll out and it is slower to see the fruit of it, but it is an important thing to do because of the times the church finds itself in. He pointed to the example of one fellow in their congregation who is incredibly gifted in taking opportunities to speak the gospel into situations. He has become a great resource in terms of "equipping other people to think about how it is to have conversational evangelism work in those spaces and to not be fearful in that space".

Underlying all this, for the Senior Pastor of 'N' Church, is the conviction that God's word does the work. He wants to give people the confidence to know that:

> . . . if faith comes through hearing and hearing through the word
> of God, then you could run all of the different things that might

be attractional and engagement and have a wonderful social conscience. But if we're not actually taking the word to people and allowing people to connect with that in ways that are biblical and relevant, then there's a kind of spinning of the wheels.

Ultimately, the Senior Pastor of 'N' Church has learnt to trust the faithful proclamation of the word, recognising that it's going to do what God intends it to do, that the church is Jesus' bride, and that he as a pastor needs to keep focused on what it means to be faithful in carrying out the ministry that God has entrusted to him.

Community Gatekeepers

In the methodological process, we highlighted some reasons for interviewing local community "gatekeepers", defined as those who have had a significant association within the community either as volunteers in some capacity, or as a long-term resident or a local business owner. These are the people whose knowledge of the suburb has been gleaned over a period of time by virtue of their standing within the community. For our purposes, we interviewed a local business owner (barista), the president of a Surf Life Saving Club, a local long-term resident with a background in media and communications and a local long-term resident who has served as a Shire Councillor and also for a term as Mayor. All four had a good local knowledge and a strong grasp of the different cultures of the Cronulla coastal context, which enabled our research to paint a picture that provides good insights and 'ways in' to be able to engage in a more intentional way.

Local Business Owner

This local barista grew up in an Italian family with a strong focus on family and music. "For me music is my spirituality and that's how I reflect on being the person I'm meant to be."

He wasn't originally from Cronulla but moved into the area. His Italian Roman Catholic Church background comes through in much of what he says—perhaps even his view of the Scriptures/the Bible as something from which you can extract good lessons: "you read the book to become a better person and go, "okay, I'll get that" and extract what you need."

As with many people, life, family and work all get in the way of a deeper spirituality.

He opened an espresso bar in 2002 at a time when Sydney had seen significant cosmopolitan change post the 2000 Summer Olympic Games. The establishment was well-received right from the outset, and it has become a Cronulla institution. He believes it was a case of the right thing at the right time, especially as more money was coming into the area, which was bringing with it a different kind of clientele.

Over the years he has observed that lifestyle in the area is a big thing: in his eyes it has morphed from what you wore and going out perhaps once a week to eating out 3-4 times a week and frequenting coffee shops perhaps 3-4 times a day. Many of his customers he finds are "using it as their office". This going out more has even extended to those 'red letter' days. Mother's Day, Father's Day and ANZAC Day are all busy days, but "the general public are going out for that family ritualistic event," where the cultural shift has seen people spending money on each other on those days because it is now part of the lifestyle.

He observes the cycle of people at work followed by leisure time—with the focus of recreation/leisure on going out. He says, "Instead of being at home and bringing friends over, they're going to the local café and bringing friends there or meeting up there and making new friends."

What was most fascinating was how he ascribed a secular liturgy of sorts to his business. He observes,

> . . . My shop is even looked at as a local . . . temple or a church . . . because people congregate [he gets what church is]. And yeah, it's over a cup of coffee which becomes the medium. That coffee is almost like the unreadable word to bring people together.

For many people, this espresso bar is your classic Third Place: as a community hub, it has generated a significant cult following within the suburb for the 17 years it has been operating. The owner finds it hard to articulate some of the cultural aspects but in amongst what he describes as the "rollercoaster" of operating a business, people have always felt magnetized to the place: " . . . it could be because of the coffee . . . because of the coffee community that's there, or meeting new friends or doing business." For the owner, "it's about spreading a message of people", which for him is something that has been passed onto him through his family. It is also for him being part of something: "I've always craved to be part of something and what I've done on the flipside of that is created something that people feel they want to be a part of, and that is where the success is." This builds into the belonging and community aspect or as Dietrich Bonhoeffer puts it, that "life together", which is an integral part of the community of God's people.

He sees success in creating something that people feel they either need or feel part of, which has in turn become something people feel they can belong to. And for him, while the financial aspect is certainly important, he takes great joy in people coming.

The espresso bar has become "the modern-day version of a church", as James K. A. Smith puts it.[16] There's a secular liturgy attached to this. One could describe the liturgy of it in this way:

"You go in there, you meet friends . . . it's their first calling card of the day. They get greeted with a smile. They get called by their first name—they're known. It's where people have made friends. Relationships have come from it, people have had their wedding photos taken there. When a couple has a baby, "the first thing they want to do is send me photos of them wearing a baby jumpsuit that says "Grind" on it."

When pushed on how he's created this culture, he speaks of it as:

> . . . just a series of events of being able to care for people and under-
> stand that coffee might be that five minutes of their life but there's
> so much more. It's that person who can teach me something, and
> I can hopefully teach them something over the medium being a
> cup of coffee.

What they have been able to create in a suburban coastal context, with an overabundance of coffee shops and a famous beach on the doorstep, is an extraordinary culture and community. Indeed 17 years means, in summary, for this barista: "I am nothing without them . . . and they feel a part of something, they feel they belong to something without me or the product".

The conversation shifted towards his take on people's view of church and at times the apathy displayed towards it. Responding to this apathy, he sees it as something ingrained in the culture of our modern world. People are just engrossed in their own life, which seeps into how people think (or don't think) about church. An interesting observation he makes is that in times of trouble, people still turn to the church.

He also pointed to some of the more classic (or "old-school") community involvement.

16. Smith, *You Are What You Love*, 42-46.

The writer developed a good relationship with this barista and had his guitar trio play live in the church building as a way of showcasing the acoustics but, more importantly, as a means for people who had never set foot in our building to come and enjoy some live music. As a "light reach" entry point, a short gospel-shaped talk was a feature of each evening.

There's an understanding he shows of the once central place the church occupied in cities, in towns and in people's thinking. This led him to ask the question about what churches ought to be doing. He suggests it's like it needs to be a new order—for how the church can become that focal point again in places like Cronulla where you have the beach and a popular local footy team, alongside parks, restaurants and cafés which is all so lifestyle- driven. Incredibly, the interview got him self-reflecting on why he couldn't even give just one hour of his week to church, given that he probably spends an hour scrolling through Instagram. He muses, "What is God asking, one hour a week to think of me and what I've done to set up humanity . . . How many people got (sic.) a 2000-year-old legacy? Not many . . . "

As he reflected on the cultural shift for churches and how they can get back into focus, he asked good questions about what draws people (attraction). Do churches need to open coffee shops? How does the church become part of the lifestyle (the cultural social fabric of the suburb)? The focus on lifestyle within the interview led him to ponder these questions further.

What this meant is that people no longer find their sanctuary in the church, but in other lifestyles. He wonders whether there will be some kind of impetus that will see people go back to it, since the modern-day lifestyle is about creating places for people to get together at restaurants or coffee shops "since the rest of their social fix is social media."

Community Organisation—Former President, Cronulla SLSC

Our interviewee has been active for the last 25 years in the Cronulla SLSC and as a volunteer, he has spent 22 years managing the life-saving equipment. He is strongly career-focused but this is balanced with a strong devotion to surfing and water sports. Our interview based on the questions in Appendix 5 gave him pause for reflection on a number of life aspects. Sundays for his family was a home-focused family day; when his kids were younger it was a beach day.

His dad took him to church on Sunday mornings (though there was not much talk around religion at home). Being raised as a Roman Catholic, he went to a Catholic school and he and his wife have followed a similar tradition with their children.

Once older, he would go surfing with his mates in the morning and then go to a 6pm service on a Sunday night, describing it in this way: "It was *your* Sunday." Church was something partially on the radar, though he points out that he went along with his then girlfriend (now his wife) to accompany her. "But I just decided one day I didn't need it . . . I just didn't need to go and sit in church." He says,

> . . . a lot of people have decided that they won't go to church be-
> cause all those things that have now become available on Sundays
> and the shift in family practices and people's social practices has
> come down to the availability of other options . . . people have
> become very self-focused.

He went on to note, "It's surprising how many people probably would think that they still have some religious beliefs but just don't practice them by going to church, just because people have become very self-focused culturally." This actually means that they have become very self-focused spiritually. It is now "*my* spirituality", which isn't influenced by anyone or anything else.

Our conversation focused also on the issue of being time-poor, which he thinks is really just an excuse since people generally have the choice of how they're going to spend their time. He wonders also whether many people were once "borderline churchgoers"—brought up in churchgoing families but arrived at a stage where with pressures around they didn't necessarily want to be viewed in that light and their response was to stop going to church.

Interestingly, this led him to focus on the question of whether he really needed to go to church and instead the beach has become that point of spirituality for him. He says, "I used to surf every day . . . and I'd actually think of that later on when I was thinking about religion. I was on this wave . . . they call it "the green cathedral."" His mantra when signing off in the weekly Surf Club newsletters became "Where else would you rather be?" It is this secular liturgy of the surf which I explore more in the final chapter.

While he picked up on significant changes in the physical nature of Cronulla—congestion, proliferation of high-rise and medium density buildings, shift in the shops from speciality stores to cafés /restaurants—the suburb in his eyes has retained its distinct culture that crosses boundaries.

He noted that "so much of people's life is based around the beach and the bays." Furthermore, the shift in trading hours changed the make-up of people who frequent Cronulla on the weekends.

When asked to comment on the role that churches play in the life of a suburb, he saw them as being "a community within the community". Having always been a strong advocate of community, given his volunteer role within the Surf Club, he sees the church's role as having an ongoing importance, though in a limited way since he displayed that classic view of Christianity as being about morals and ethics. At church he enjoyed talks that related the Scriptures to everyday life "rather than continually saying, remember Jesus did this and he did that for you . . . it was more, Jesus did this, but there's a message there for your life." It is our contention that this is clearly something churches need to be even more conscious of and intentional about when it comes to teaching the Bible.

In seeking to capture some of the elements of a secular community like this one, we were able to glean some observations around the strength of the Surf Life Saving community. He pointed out that any community ought to have a sense of belonging—noting that there's always a commonality when it comes to what you believe in or how one ought to contribute towards the life of that community. Herein lies where a religious community will obviously be different to a sporting community. What unites people when it comes to a church community is their Christian belief and practice, while in the Surf Club it starts with the lifestyle, the location and a range of activities. But the common theme is still that connection between people, and like a church there's a common goal. The Surf Life Saving Club, while being a community service organisation, shares a similarity with a church community in that they're seeking, amongst other aims, to serve their community. Their motivations are different, but that is also their liturgy: they're there to serve the community, to get fit, to train the next generation of Surf Life Savers, to foster those bonds and to train to compete as they encourage members to take their involvement to the next level. Interestingly, he pointed out that the problem comes when they lose sight of why they are members of a SLSC in the first place: saving lives and giving back into the community.

As a result, " . . . people get a great deal of satisfaction or reward, feel an obligation to contribute because that is how the club operates."

Thus, with an SLSC you have a community "full of people with similar interests or passions [who] get the same satisfaction out of a lot of their activities . . . those who are selfless and contribute . . . [but also] those who see it as an avenue to achieve something they personally want".

As was alluded to above, like a church community there is a commonality amongst those who know what their focus is. There's a sense of belonging attached to that: he says, "the commonality of interests and then the community service or other things you can get out of an organisation like that, make you want to be part of it as well."

Over the years, Surf Clubs have had to adapt; they're not immune to having a small group who don't always "buy-in" to the ideals or the culture. He points to self-focused behaviour in society as something that the club culture isn't necessarily immune to.

With different groups in the Club when it comes to certain disciplines (surf sports; patrol; overall lifesaving focus), often members will see the Club as the avenue to achieve what they want personally without necessarily giving of their time in volunteering for activities beyond their discipline.

Like church communities, they seem to struggle with transition points between certain age groups, and like church communities, a focus on the youth coming through is necessary for the development of the Club.

But what seems to set the community of Cronulla SLSC apart from some church communities is the sense of belonging that people have and that for many it is their Third Place. Many members speak of it as *their* club and will do more than just come for their thing and go home—they find great satisfaction in general involvement or contributing and just "being there".

As a general observation, churches have for some time faced the problem of the 80-20 principle with 80% of the work being carried out by 20% of the members. This President says that is not the case at Cronulla SLSC and certainly the 'clubby culture' up and down the beaches would attest to that, particularly when you see the level of involvement in everything from patrols to carnivals, training and committees.

It is our contention that the culture of Surf Life Saving clubs has much to say to churches when it comes to levels of involvement and the desire to be a solid part of the community.

Furthermore, it is clear that Surf Life Saving clubs are that "Third Place" which Oldenburg spoke of and that they also have a liturgy of their own which (though with some significant differences), shares similarities to that of churches. That's why I explore these secular liturgies of the beach and the culture of Surf Life Saving Clubs in the next chapter, in order to be more intentional about how churches can speak the truth, beauty and liveability of the gospel into the lives of those who are deeply enmeshed in communities. In the words of our interviewee,

> Clearly, I think people feel there's a place for the church, but their involvement is the thing that may be an interesting challenge . . . I think there's a lot of people think that they had belief and to some degree accepted religion, but they just don't practice it as much, or in the same way that their parents did, or even maybe when they were much younger.

This highlights again just how much we find ourselves in a post-Christian world. While there was once a general acceptance of the Christian narrative of redemptive history and church membership was not seen as a hindrance for participation in society, all of that needs to be rethought in this post-Christian era. The refrain particularly from those interviewed who once did go to church (albeit because it was "what you did") has shifted to the question of whether one really needs to go at all.

Local Councillor (and former Mayor)

Current local Councillor, wedding celebrant and former Mayor grew up in the Roman Catholic tradition and was brought up to believe in God. Prayers were a particularly important thing when growing up, from the influence of her mother, and even now she still finds comfort in saying prayers. They went to church on a Sunday because, "It's what you did on a Sunday".

Life for her in the suburb was, in her words, "fantastic"—they lived within walking distance of the beach and her parents owned a local kiosk next to the Surf Life Saving Club:

> Things were quite good and then of course, our lifestyle, we had lots of friends, we used to go boating, belong (sic) to the Royal Motor Yacht Club . . . It was a great community. Cronulla was a wonderful place to bring up children.

Her church upbringing is not something that has been passed on to her children. They went to Sunday school for a while, but then they didn't want to go, preferring to spend time with their friends.

These days she will go to church now and then. Because of her Council work she represents different churches, and when they ask her to go, "I always feel nice when I come out of church". However for her, life has changed quite a bit and there's certainly no drive for it to be part of her everyday life.

She recounted the significant changes she has seen from the days when Cronulla was this sleepy little seaside village, to the bustling business district it has become today. Coupled with that is the proliferation of units that now pepper the streets of Cronulla, particularly near the beach. She observed that the area is ageing as retirees swap their bigger houses up the line for multi-million-dollar units.

Furthermore, she notes the change in how families operate. With the desire to live in a coastal context like Cronulla, families will do whatever they can to make this happen, to the point where:

> most people today . . . can't afford for mum to stay at home, she's got to work. So I think things have changed there. Everyone seems to have two or three jobs. The kids are in childcare. Everyone comes home from work and they're all exhausted.

In the conversation surrounding lifestyle, she observed the challenge of teenagers who seem to have nowhere to go these days and end up sometimes in trouble. She would like to see churches offer more to young people, but doesn't think that church is inviting enough these days. This led to a discussion about the kinds of things that were happening for her growing up in school. She believes that the church needs to offer more social activities to draw young people back. She thinks churches and particularly the churches of Cronulla aren't visually out there enough, noting that at the Spring Festival "you never see the churches come down there with a little kiosk." Interestingly, a number of times she made the point that churches need to get out into the community more and get involved where they can and have a presence.

She believes the church needs to offer more youth-oriented programs with special nights for young people to come and listen with music. Her suggestions included getting some of the players from the Cronulla Rugby League team to come to the church and do a meet and greet, knowing that some of them are Christians. After all, "they're so impressed with footballers, aren't they?"

When asked about where the church sits within the community and in people's consciousness, she pointed to the problem of institutional child abuse within the churches in general but with Catholicism in particular. But again and again, the issue seemed to come back to people's lack of time and busyness that she says is ridiculous but needs to be acknowledged for what it is.

In the end, as we've observed, there are so many different things for people to do these days, and for many, church or religion, which was once a big part of people's lives has faded into the background as just one option among many or sadly, not an option at all.

These days her faith is, like other "spiritual but not necessarily religious" people, an infusion of ideas. She loves the stories of the Bible, loves visiting churches overseas, and when pressed about her belief, she said:

> . . . see, I choose to believe in God. I get a lot of comfort out of thinking; things are meant to be, something's looking after you and if you live a good life and you're good to people, it will come back to you. I've always believed in karma, and I think that you just get so much out of doing that little bit extra for people.

What Can We Observe?

As I drew together the data collected from the interviews, a number of common themes began to emerge. The correlation of these themes across the churches interviewed and also from the interviews with Cronulla locals, highlight certain commonalities along particular lines that, in my mind, hold significance when it comes to the challenges faced and steps churches have taken/ought to take to address those challenges missionally.

The intent wasn't to rank any of these findings, since each church finds itself in different circumstances. Instead, the point is to provide a set of factors that can be taken as principles which could be applied in a local context.

An intent to engage with the suburb by identifying and connecting with certain micro-cultures. It is clear from our analysis that churches which had identified and sought to connect in a meaningful way with particular micro-cultures were experiencing some sort of growth. For example, 'M2' Church and 'P' Church both serve their local primary schools in an intentional way: 'M2' Church by way of a "Backyard Blitz" initiative which has built their reputation as a different place. The school couldn't believe they were doing it. The conversation transpired in this way:

> You're paying for this?" I said, "yeah". He said, "Why?" I said, "because we believe in God and we believe God loves people and I

want to give tangible expression to that in the community. And how we are known is very important . . . I want us to be known as a people who love people . . .

In the same vein, as I outlined in the qualitative findings, 'P' Church did a similar thing by running a coffee cart at school market days and a parent open day (by invitation of the principal). They donated the money taken from the coffee cart back to the school as a way of being a blessing to their community.

The beauty about this kind of faithful presence is that it doesn't match up with people's paradigm of what they think of church. But it's not just connecting as the findings show, it is also making those bold decisions which enable churches to move a step further along.

This leads us to explore further what kind of missional advantage there is for churches in these suburban coastal contexts that enjoy a village style and how congregations can harness that village "vibe". For it is in these village contexts that people come to know one another and there are many long-term residents. Thus, in a culture where sometimes ministers (or anyone perhaps who moves into one of these suburban coastal contexts) are not really considered residents until they've been living there a number of years, it is important to put the hard yards in and adopt that faithful presence for the long-haul.

This led to another common theme: **that a deep understanding of the area is important.** Every church I interviewed had a reasonably strong understanding of their area when it came to demographics, cultural and sociological issues. They had worked hard at utilising the statistics from the National Church Life Survey which enabled them to tailor a specific approach to mission in their suburb. But while that work had been done, for some there is still a disconnect between the statistics and insights which NCLS provide and a way of leveraging that for mission.

It is important for church leaders to provide opportunities for church members to get to know their suburbs really well. There is a level of cultural naivety when it comes to some church members' understanding of their areas and their realisation of the current cultural climate. This highlights the importance of ministry teams and senior ministers setting the tone and leading the way in not just getting to know their suburb but communicating ways in which they're doing that for their congregation members and providing opportunities for them to get involved as well. As one Rector put it,

> I was surprised at how little I learnt [from existing members] except sitting somewhere that they lived and them giving me distant observations about [the area] . . . mostly these guys couldn't show me their tribe; their tribe was church.

Outreach through identifying "touchpoints". Churches that identified and targeted certain "points of vulnerability" or specific "touchpoints" give themselves good opportunity and connection from which to build bridges of connection into their Sunday gatherings. This is highlighted by recognising that the micro-cultures of the Surf Clubs or schools provide a basic inroad into the community, but then also harnessing those felt needs in the community (marriage, parenting, and even mental health) and working out how best to provide practical support as well allow them to have that "Jesus encounter" by bringing the gospel to bear in their situation where appropriate.

Historical factors seem to have a significant impact upon where churches find themselves struggling to connect with the suburb. The bold decision by 'A' Church to purchase and convert an old RSL building into an adaptable space for ministry and mission allowed them to grow as a church and connect with the community by way of the space they set aside ("The Hub").

Strong histories of biblical focus and missional culture mean that even when a new minister arrives, that ministry/cultural DNA is something that is already embedded within the life of the church. That pre-existing culture allows a church to focus on the core business of mission.

SLS/Nippers/sporting groups involvement. It's clear from the findings that four of the churches that were interviewed had some kind of formal involvement in the local Surf Life Saving Club.

Two churches have taken deliberate steps to create a church time that fits with the Nippers culture and those two churches have seen significant growth. One church had tried to run a service at a later timeslot but due to a lack of resourcing, buy-in and perhaps vision, they weren't able to get it off the ground. Two churches highlighted the importance of members being involved in the life of the Surf Clubs rather than churches trying to create a space for meeting in the Clubs themselves. According to one pastor who was interviewed, meeting in the Surf Club made the relationship between the church and the Club a tricky one by virtue of it being a shared space.

My findings show a number of the churches seek to **harness key yearly events as "missional moments"**. These are ways of building bridges from the community to church and when harnessed by being followed by a course (e.g., Alpha, Christianity Explored/Explained) there is great potential for the gospel to pierce people's hearts. This has for a long time been a strength of churches, however as I will explore in Chapter 5 when we consider the place of discipleship in the local church, it is necessary in this post-Christian environment to shift the mindset from running events for the sake of it to equipping our people to think more broadly about ministry. One such example might be to consider utilising their small groups as "missional communities".[17]

Coupled with these factors is the observation across the board that churches in these suburban coastal contexts are hampered by particular cultural factors. Most (if not all) of the suburbs in which these churches are located have an aspirational bent. Certainly we discovered the Northern Beaches were described by a number of the ministers as a "destination"; that is, there is a strong desire to be able to live there as a family or to retire there. This idea of destination stems from the idyllic nature of these areas having a "heaven on earth" feel, such that for many people they will say, "This is kind of heaven on earth and so why would I need anything beyond that?" More to the point, why do people need Jesus if this really is the ultimate? Chapter 5 will offer some ways forward on this, but briefly to (a) help people reorder their disordered loves since, the "contest of cultural practices is a competition for one's heart"[18] and (b) show them that what Jesus offers is infinitely better in the context of worship, relationships and a church community that backs this up.

The myriad of leisure opportunities that come with the lifestyle of suburban coastal contexts gives churches the feeling of irrelevance: the church is largely forgotten because the suburbs are such good places in which to live.

Sometimes it's these cultural factors that end up spilling over into the life and culture of the church. For four of the churches there is a challenge as they seek to connect with what the Senior Minster of 'A' Church described as the "relaxed coastal types". A certain non-committal attitude has found its way into some of these churches, meaning that the culture of the suburban coastal context is more laid-back which has the tendency to

17. At the time of writing, COVID-19 leaves a cloud of uncertainty hanging over these types of events and so within the current climate our churches are needing to think differently about how we can best utilise Christmas 2020 and perhaps even Easter 2021.

18. Smith, *You Are What You Love*, 22.

make people more unreliable. As one pastor recalled in an interview, the observation of a staff member on congregational attitudes was: "if I come to church, I might come to church but if I don't it's no big deal" (Senior Minister, 'A' Church). Another Rector acknowledged the difficulty with engaging people in regular roles in ministry due to the *laissez-faire* approach to church coupled with an over-commitment to other areas of life, particularly an ultra-involvement in the lives of their children.

We joke about people turning up late for church, but he surmised it was more marked in this area and that making a commitment to a church service is more difficult. A greater reluctance was noticed in the 20-30 age bracket.

He ended by pointing out, " . . . somehow in a beachside suburb where it is more relaxed as you walk along—that affects how you think of your discipleship."

Therefore, it is worth pondering how churches are discipling their members when it comes to engaging with the community, making disciples, and decisions they make in terms of church and gathering with God's people—how they're being trained and equipped for ministry so as to be able to reach out courageously in their relevant spheres of influence.

Thus, seasonal tensions with families juggling extra-curricular activities and confronting that relaxed coastal 'non-committal' attitude which has rubbed off on people in church, needs also to be an area of focus. And it perhaps comes back to discipleship: helping people in our churches through sustained Bible teaching and training (remembering that important shift in thinking from programs to people). Having a "Vine" mindset means helping people to have a more gospel-focused mindset as they rub shoulders with people within their spheres of influence.

Church Culture/DNA is also a factor. The Senior Minister of 'M2' Church pointed to a longevity of ministry that can shape a church: "where if you keep teaching and pastoring well and gospelling, you would expect to see growth. If you think the gospel is the power of God, you should see something happening". It is clear, however, that this may not always be the case as the Rector at 'C' Church would attest to. His sentiment is the same but the results have been markedly different. It is clear that the intentionality of gospel-focused initiatives and the cultural DNA of the church has a significant impact upon the types of ministry initiatives that are undertaken.

Similarly, the ministry or cultural DNA of 'A' Church meant that bold, courageous decisions were made in a "forward-thinking", "future-oriented" and "outward-focused" way. That debate between tradition and future orientation which many churches have at some stage, in this case had a significant bearing on where 'A' Church now finds itself placed with a strong missional DNA. It is of note that in the midst of this strategic decision-making, 'A' Church was also asked to take responsibility for the smaller more traditional church in the suburb next door that found itself on a trajectory of decline with little financial viability.

Historically, this was important to the mission and direction of 'A' Church. There are strengths and weaknesses of amalgamations. However the minister pointed out that with their branch church having a distinctly more traditional Anglican expression of church life that perhaps the main centre didn't have, it meant they were able to direct those who desired that expression of churchmanship to the branch church. This in the end allowed 'A' Church greater permission to keep moving forward with a strong missional focus.

Demographically, we have found that it is not uncommon to have a high proportion of apartment dwellings in these areas which can make it difficult to reach people. And while the high cost of living means many of these areas have a high level of transience for their churches, it can also provide churches with some high net-worth individuals who are of great benefit to gospel partnership.

In all of this it is still important to ask, what is it that churches aren't doing that they could be doing to communicate to people that Jesus is better; that gathering with God's people is better. It is clear that for some churches, the Sunday afternoon timeslot has worked as a service time, but there are still other factors to take into consideration, including the vision that was shown to the congregation members and the subsequent level of buy-in and the resources that they have to do this while keeping a Sunday morning gathering viable.

As one Senior Minister asked, "What is it that needs to happen?" Certainly, there needs to be an experience of faith, a movement of the Holy Spirit which causes people to say Jesus is Lord—not just intellectually, but in their hearts. In the next chapter as we look at ways forward, I will suggest some ways in which this could be possible, particularly along the lines of showing people that Jesus is the one who can reorder their "disordered love and devotion", since we practice our way into idolatries, absorbing them from the water in which we swim. Hence our idolatries often reflect the ethos of our environments. For there is a truth, a beauty and a liveability to the gospel that ought to be clearly articulated in our evangelistic endeavours which will, God-willing, reorder people's desires and hopes from what disappoints to what brings true satisfaction.

In the end we also we need to remember that God brings the growth. In the words of one minister,

> . . . you know it's going to be tough but it's not until you've been there that you actually know that it's going to be tough, till you've experienced it . . . I've learned that there's a greater dependence on God than there was before, the experience has brought me to a deeper dependence on Him, and in the end that's Christian ministry.

Interestingly, in the midst of the struggles and challenges, it was important to be reminded that the one thing that must remain at the core of our thinking is the power of the gospel to transform people's lives. It's a good reminder that there's no silver bullet, for there is no substitution for the power of God's Word (*the* silver bullet). Everything else we do is ancillary to that.

7

Where Do We Go from Here?

All God's children say
What did they say?
They just want heaven on a stick

All God's children say
What did they say?
They just want heaven on a stick

We don't need opinion sways
Nowhere to run
Just wanna see those blue green bays

James Reyne, *Heaven on a Stick*, 1987

THE LYRICS TO THIS quintessentially Australian song summarize much of what I unearthed in my research and the attitudes of those living in the suburban coastal contexts of the Sydney metropolitan area: it is the good life. The suburbs in beachside areas of Sydney are where people go to pursue a comfortable, secure, settled life—it's a destination. For some, it may be for a good time and not necessarily a long time. For others, they are areas to pursue their dreams. There is a lifestyle that accompanies it, where people are 'laid-back' but also strongly motivated when it comes to pursuing that lifestyle. For many, it provides them with the chance to live out their long-held aspirational values. Indeed for many it's about the status of their area often coupled with a strong sense of tribalism. There is also a sense that those living in these contexts are there as a result of their hard work.

Within this secular hedonism there is very little perceived need for God. Those who may give some assent to God or admit to some kind of belief, only do so because they see religion as perhaps serving the purpose of having blessed their aspirations or having played a part in their fulfilment.[1]

Hence the good life has become the "cultural narrative" that many in these suburban coastal contexts have embraced. Therefore, as we think about the place of the church within beachside contexts, it is the gospel that can offer a new vision of the good life for those who have embraced that cultural narrative.[2] As a long-term Cronulla resident put it:

> Quite often for people from the outside looking in on the beach-side communities, they're seen as homogenous, but they're not: they're quite diverse. But one could move from the context of Cronulla, to the far North Coast of NSW and it's a very different socioeconomic mix. While in Cronulla, there's a strong concentration of people over the age of 65, and similarly the far North Coast with a lot of retirees, there are still pockets of the North Coast displaying some of the highest unemployment rates.

So, what do churches do in those contexts? Who do they reach out to and how do they reach out to those groups? Where ought a church target their resources, time and effort? It's important therefore to ask what the rationale and the criteria is behind that. More often than not, it's where the emphasis falls on what one believes is the centrepiece of church life, whether it's evangelism, whether it's worship, whether it's pastoral or whether it's teaching. And that will drive, a lot of the time, what churches do.

By way of a preliminary comment, it is important to note as I put forward some strategies and offer suggestions on ways forward, that there is no man-made 'silver bullet' when it comes to reaching into these suburban coastal contexts. As a couple of pastors reminded me, we must keep coming back to what we believe about the effectual nature of God's word. It does not return empty (Rom 11), it is living and active (Heb 4:12); the gospel is God's power for the salvation of all who believe (Rom 1:16). As Christians first and foremost, we see this happen as God's people gather, as his word is preached and God's people are built up, equipped and strengthened by his Spirit for the task of going out into the world.

We have also seen that most, if not all of the churches surveyed are already involved in word-based ministry that seeks to reach their areas with

1. Foster, *Suburban Captivity*, 77.
2. Foster, *Suburban Captivity*, 77.

the gospel. The harvest is plentiful, but the soil is hard-going. More often than not it feels as though people are impervious to the good news of life offered in Jesus and the promise of eternal life in God's Kingdom, when all they can see in front of them is as close to heaven as they can perceive. As C. S. Lewis brilliantly captured it in his sermon, *The Weight of Glory*:

> . . . if we consider the unblushing promises of reward and the staggering nature of the rewards promised in the Gospels, it would seem that Our Lord finds our desires, not too strong, but too weak. We are half-hearted creatures, fooling about with drink and sex and ambition when infinite joy is offered us, like an ignorant child who wants to go on making mud pies in a slum because he cannot imagine what is meant by the offer of a holiday at the sea. We are far too easily pleased.[3]

Alongside the atomising effects of technology, the progressive intellectual movement and the movement of popular culture against Christianity, the most significant challenge in Australia remains a sustained affluence. It contains, as one Australian socio-political commentator puts it, "an especially alluring falsehood—the idea that some people don't need God's mercy".[4]

But as I alluded to earlier, there is still amongst some Australians a religious bent. In a nationwide survey undertaken in 2017, McCrindle research found that 45% of Australians identify with Christianity broadly while 55% identifying also as "non religious" still captured a spirituality. Within that, 14% identified as 'spiritual but not religious' (McCrindle 2017, 7). The survey showed that religion in Australia is far from dead: in fact two thirds of Australians (68%) currently follow a religion or have spiritual beliefs. This is significant because when as we look at spirituality and religion, 61% are attracted by people who live out a genuine faith.

This means there are a number of inroads that can be made with the gospel into the cultural fabric of suburban coastal contexts. This chapter will pick up on some ways forward and draw upon the insights of some people who can help us.

3. Lewis, *Weight of Glory*.
4. Sheridan, *God is Good for You*, 23.

Where do we go from here?

As we gather a number of the threads together from our biblical-theological survey and qualitative research, there are three areas of focus worth highlighting in helping churches build on their current ministries or re-think their strategies as they seek to connect in a meaningful way that will show people the truth, beauty and goodness of the gospel. This final chapter focuses on these areas which it is hoped will be of use to churches in other suburban coastal contexts. These are obviously general, and specific applications have to be made depending on particular contexts, but my hope is that the framework on the whole is a helpful one for the hedonistic, aspiration-driven areas. So let's consider what it could look like to embrace an urban spirituality; how we can show those around us what it looks like to "reorder their disordered loves"; and how by way of stronger discipleship we can encourage church members to foster a faithful presence in their spheres of influence.

Embracing an Urban Spirituality—recapturing the "Nones"

In Chapter 2 I established the challenge Australia has faced for some years now but was brought to light in the 2016 Census with the rise of the "spiritual but not religious" and particularly those who now identify with "no religion".

Chapter 3 highlighted the need (through the important work of Newbigin, Keller and more recently James K. A. Smith) and the importance for Christians to seek to embrace a cultural transformation by way of contextualisation, as well as establishing a "faithful presence" in their spheres of influence.

Most Christian people spend time amongst unbelievers, but as I've established there's a risk in ministry that we're not doing this and indeed that perhaps it's not being modelled as well as ministers would hope to amongst their church members. We must resist both the temptation to withdraw and to conform. We have these great pressures because we "like to be liked" but our neighbours' eternal prosperity is more important.

As we seek to recast a true spirituality for our communities, it's worth considering what this could look like in the urban/suburban coastal context. In her book entitled *Urban Spirituality: Embodying God's Mission in the Neighbourhood*, Karina Kreminski posits a helpful way forward as one possible counter to the spiritual "Nones" who are all around us.

Recognising that the church in the West needs to see itself as being located in a mission field, Kreminski argues that instead of a spirituality that is more about withdrawing from the world, we ought to be focusing on engaging with it. Of course, this isn't anything new and the research over the years, the myriad of books and the conversations we have had with other pastors highlight that very point. However, it is one thing to have read so many books or attended various conferences; it's another to actually be able to establish a framework and even provide some kind of roadmap to help guide us in these times.

What then, makes reaching the "Nones" or those who don't see how church connects with Jesus/Christianity so difficult? One challenge faced by the church in Australia and other Western countries is not the rise in unbelief. Certainly in the Sutherland Shire of Sydney it is also not antagonistic atheism. Rather it is the sharp rise in recent years of a belief detached from an idea of belonging.

Sociologists describe this phenomenon as "unusually low levels of active religiousness living alongside relatively high levels of nominal belief." I've already shown how much of the previous "Anglican" self-identification was very nominal. It would be true of all the major denominations and given this nominal nature, it is the most prone to decay.

These nominals would fit into one or more of the categories that Drescher outlines in *Choosing our Religion*. Certainly amongst the nominal Anglicans with whom I cross paths, many would class themselves as spiritual but not religious, even where they've had some kind of religious upbringing, either in going along to Sunday school with their parents when they were younger, or from their schools.

The main approach I wish to suggest, given the analysis of our research when it comes to embracing more of an urban spirituality[5] is considering the peculiarities and the 'touchpoints' or points of vulnerability that are part of the social fabric of many communities.

---

5. Cities have many characteristics—Urban Spirituality (according to Kreminski) can be defined as reflecting on one's city and urbanism from God's perspective (21). That is, instead of a spirituality that has tended to lean more towards "withdrawing rather than engaging" and "individualistic rather than communal", the church needs to embrace a spirituality which recognises it is located in a mission field with all the cultural attachments that go with that and joins in God's mission as a "way of life" (33).

Hirsch contends that mission is an extension or by-product of a spirituality based on Jesus and what we see of how he went about engaging people in the Gospels. Jesus saw the points of vulnerability and he spoke into them. In shaping our missional engagement therefore, it makes sense to engage people where they are at in a meaningful and attentive way. This was a focal point of St Andrew's Cronulla's *Mission 2023* document crafted in 2018 which had four interconnected objectives. Engaging with the suburb was one of these objectives with the desire to connect in a meaningful way with the community through ministry initiatives including, but not limited to, an integrated wedding ministry along with targeted seminars and workshops that speak directly into touchpoints including marriage enrichment, various parenting courses and divorce care.[6] Our conversations with other churches revealed specific attempts to engage with points of vulnerability in their suburbs in a way that sees a spirituality patterned on Jesus.

In a similar fashion to Hirsch, Kreminski outlines an urban spirituality that is "oriented around the *missio Dei* or the mission of God". She suggests that we ought to be asking the question, "What is God up to in my city?"[7] This relies on an understanding that God has already gone ahead of us and so it's up to us to discern where the Spirit is active and then connect with his mission. In my research I discovered this framed as "points of vulnerability" where churches need to be identifying (and many already are) those "touchpoints" in the community where one can speak the gospel into people's lives, spending time with those outside of the faith who are yearning for community, meaning and hope. One long-term Cronulla resident and Christian expressed it in the following way:

> You look at Jesus a lot of the time; it was the Ministry of Interruption. Because people were at a point of vulnerability. And the lady who grabs his cloak that's got the bleeding problem. The person

---

6. At the time of writing much of this was put on hold due to the COVID-19 pandemic; the restrictions imposed on many areas of life and ministry across New South Wales (particularly the suspension of church gatherings) but also the departure of the writer from St Andrew's Cronulla in July 2020 to take up the position of Senior Minister at the Anglican Church in Seaforth on Sydney's Northern Beaches. It is hoped at the time of writing that as social restrictions are gradually eased and as the writer takes up this new ministry position that some of these ideas and concepts gleaned from the research as well as the lessons learnt and experiences from ten years of ministry in Cronulla will after a time of observation and cultural exegesis be utilised over the ministry in the long term.

7. Kreminski, *Urban Spirituality*, 35.

who's blind comes and, Jesus says to them your faith has made you well, and the lepers and the father who comes to him because his daughter is dying. All of these show a point of vulnerability.

Thus, we can apply this to churches in their suburban coastal contexts, as we consider the people who come into our churches, but more importantly as we consider members of our church and the relationships they have with the non-Christian people in their suburbs broadly but also in their spheres of influence more specifically.

As an example, St Andrew's Cronulla was in the early stages of harnessing the "Cronulla Anglican Op Shop" in an attempt to build on that established ministry to the community. This was seen as a way of connecting more meaningfully with those who came in and who had different needs. The idea was, as well as meeting any material needs, to offer them a community engagement course that might speak into their current life situation and then bridge that to an "explaining Christianity" course. This stemmed from the statistics from the *Faith and Belief in Australia* research showing that Australians most value the church and Christian organisations for their work with those in need. Australians highly value the work of the church in looking after people who are homeless (74% "extremely" or "somewhat value" this), offering financial assistance/food relief programs (72%) and providing disaster relief (69%).[8]

Therefore, identifying those points of vulnerability as a way of (re)connecting the church with the community can be a powerful way of showing the truth and beauty of the gospel. In fact in the early days of COVID-19, Cronulla Anglican along with a number of churches throughout Sydney in partnership with Anglicare were able to carry out food drives to offer food relief to families who needed emergency assistance. For the Anglican Church in Cronulla, they were able to partner with the local public school to provide families who were in need with food hampers who were in need, thus building on an already solid relationship with the local school but also being that beacon of light in a time of distress, uncertainty and darkness for many.

In a similar vein, of the churches I interviewed, this kind of connection has been on their agenda and it is important to note the correlation between gospel growth of these churches and the level of community engagement. For example, the way these churches captured identified touchpoints or points of vulnerability came in the form of ministry initiatives

8. McCrindle, "Faith and Belief," 10.

such as mental health courses, a weekly soup kitchen, or a regular marriage enrichment course. In some cases it has been a matter of going to where people are in shared spaces (e.g., in one interview with the owner of a local Cronulla espresso bar it was suggested that a course exploring Christianity could be run at their café (interestingly proffered by the owner)). This would be a way of connecting with people who wouldn't normally walk through the doors of a church but who may be interested in engaging with some of the deeper questions of life and faith.

Again, it is a fairly obvious point to make but in the majority of the cases there is a deep desire on the parts of the churches I talked to, to love their suburbs. One pastor expressed it as instead of trying to outdo the suburb, his church seeks to show a consistent love in the hope of "outloving them".

God uses his people in mission by sending his church into the world. And where churches are able to identify these points of vulnerability, that can be a source of blessing but also can open opportunities to bring the truth, beauty and liveability of the gospel to bear on their coastal contexts. The challenge, is to continue to work on how to build bridges into the life of the church.

Of course, there will always be aspects of culture that we dislike because they run contrary to God's plan of bringing justice, forgiveness, life and peace to our world. This is important since time and again we see the culture of our cities seeking to shape us according to the false narratives of our society.[9]

What some might label false narratives, could be coined in other ways. James K. A. Smith has fashioned this into the idea of cultural/secular liturgies. These liturgies are, he says, the sorts of practices that form us—that form our core or ultimate identities.[10] It's this topic to which I turn now.

Reordering Disordered Loves

Earlier I alluded to the cultural narrative of parts of Sydney's suburban coastal contexts. One idea that has permeated my conversations with pastors and community gatekeepers in these contexts is an underlying spirituality which the beach seems to hold, along with the notion that these suburbs are perceived as destinations holding a strong tribalism.

9. Kreminski, *Urban Spirituality*, 37.
10. Smith, *Desiring the Kingdom*, 26.

In engaging with the false cultural narratives, James K. A. Smith has done much to help us on what it looks like to be a disciple of Jesus in the post-Christian landscape. In his book *Desiring the Kingdom*, he models what he refers to as a "cultural exegesis" of our secular rituals and practices. This cultural exegesis involves asking, "What vision of human flourishing is implicit in this or that practice? What does the good life look like as embedded in cultural rituals? What sort of person will I become after being immersed in this or that cultural liturgy?"[11]

So, cultural exegesis, much like biblical apocalyptic literature, is a mode of "unmasking" or "unveiling the realities around us for what they really are."[12] Smith's hope is that "the shift of focus from ideas to practices, from beliefs to liturgy, will function as a methodological jolt that gets us into a position to see cultural practices and institutions in ways we've never seen them before."[13]

By way of example, he offers three liturgical analyses of cultural institutions by examining the mall, the stadium, and the modern university, demonstrating that "implicit in their liturgies are visions of the kingdom—visions of human flourishing—that are antithetical to the biblical vision of shalom."[14] However, even these secular liturgies point to the fact that we are liturgical animals. "Secular liturgies don't create our desire; they point it, aim it, direct it to certain ends."[15]

It is helpful as we outline a "where-to", to delve a little more deeply into Smith's foundation of cultural liturgies. Against a backdrop of seeking to re-frame an approach to education and specifically Christian education, *Desiring the Kingdom* sets out to show humans as beings who desire, more so than beings who are primarily knowing—that is, it is the heart which drives much of who are we and what we do:

> ... liturgies—whether "sacred" or "secular"—shape and constitute our identities by forming our most fundamental desires and our most basic attunement to the world. In short, liturgies make us certain kinds of people, and what defines us is what we love.[16]

11. Smith, *Desiring the Kingdom*, 89.

12. Smith, *Desiring the Kingdom*, 92.

13. Smith, *Desiring the Kingdom*, 92-93.

14. Smith, *Desiring the Kingdom*, 121.

15. Smith, *Desiring the Kingdom*, 122.

16. Smith, *Desiring the Kingdom*, 25.

To put it another way, what we desire, or love is a vision of what people think the good life looks like. This is a consistent element of our culture and while not limited to the beachside context it does form a big part in people's minds) is that of "the good life". The lifestyle that coastal contexts have to offer is one of the larger factors in the shift of people's focus and desires. As one interviewee put it, the beach was everything for him and the pull of it shapes people's actions, decisions and habits: it has become a way of life and was described as the "blue-green cathedral". It is for many their religion, their way of describing the good life in almost spiritual terms.

Smith's aim is helpful in that he takes a worldview approach, making the assumption that humans are inherently religious. In an Augustinian sense, he explains how we are essentially lovers because what we love, we worship: as teleological creatures our ultimate love is what defines us, what makes us the kind of people we are. In short, it is what we worship.[17] Smith wants to draw us away from the notion of humans as merely thinkers and point us towards humans "as more affective, embodied creatures who make our way in the world more by feeling our way around it."[18] Our ultimate loves are essentially those things that drive humans towards. and shape our vision of, the good life. Smith expresses it in this way:

> Our ultimate love is oriented by and to a picture of what we think it looks like for us to live well, and that picture then governs, shapes, and motivates our decisions and actions.[19]

Such love of course can be (and is) easily misdirected. The consequences of the Fall and the universal effect of sin stemming from it means that more often than not our ultimate desires—our loves—are aimed in the wrong direction. This is largely because, as John Calvin put it so aptly, "the human mind is, so to speak, a perpetual forge of idols"[20] or as John Piper has expressed it, a "desire factory".[21] We have exchanged the truth of God

17. Smith, *Desiring the Kingdom*, 87.

18. Smith, *Desiring the Kingdom*, 47.

19. Smith, *Desiring the Kingdom*, 53.

20. Calvin, *Institutes*, I.XI.8. Calvin goes on to say, "The human mind, stuffed as it is with presumptuous rashness, dares to imagine a god suited to its own capacity; as it labours under dullness, nay, is sunk in the grossest ignorance, it substitutes vanity and an empty phantom in the place of God. To these evils another is added. The god whom man has thus conceived inwardly he attempts to embody outwardly. The mind, in this way, conceives the idol, and the hand gives it birth."

21. Piper, *Future Grace*, 277-79.

for lies—worshipping and serving created things instead of the God who made them and gave them to us to enjoy (Rom 1:18-25).

Thus, it is within this context we find that what we love or what we direct our love or desires towards is a specific vision of "the good life" or what we think human flourishing looks like.[22]

In the suburban coastal context, there are many things that constitute "the good life" which it seems are wrapped up in a secular hedonism: pursuing and finding pleasure in what people think will satisfy them. Smith describes it this way:

> Human persons are intentional creatures whose fundamental way of 'intending' the world is love or desire. This love or desire— which is unconscious or noncognitive—is always aimed as some vision of the good life, some particular articulation of the kingdom. What primes us to be so oriented—and act accordingly—is a set of habits or dispositions that are formed in us through affective, bodily means, especially bodily practices, routines, or rituals that grab hold of our hearts through our imagination, which is closely linked to our bodily senses.[23]

None of this is detached from the real world. As Smith emphasizes, this process is not merely one that people experience as individuals, but through relationships and institutions. That is, many people's desires find their expression in and through institutions that they are connected to. Thus, humans are typically religious well before they develop any kind of theology, and formative practices cannot be reduced into mere ideas, beliefs, or doctrines. Practices, habits, and routines of worship and life shape who we are, what we love, and how we believe.

My research has established that lifestyle, a desire for belonging and community and an overall picture of the good life is what drives many people in these suburban coastal contexts.

From the assessment of my conversations, coupled with a deeper understanding of what makes people tick, and building on the work of missiologists and other cultural analysts, it's clear that part of addressing some of the hurdles for gospel growth (which some churches are already doing) begins by focusing on and addressing the desires surrounding human flourishing and the good life, to channel them into a desire for God.

---

22. Smith, *Desiring the Kingdom*, 52.

23. Smith, *Desiring the Kingdom*, 62-63.

To describe one approach the church could take on this, Smith makes a distinction between "thick" (meaningful) and "thin" (mundane) practices. Although this distinction may at times be somewhat blurry, its purpose is to emphasize that "no habit or practice is neutral."[24] Furthermore, it is important to remember that some practices that may superficially seem "thin" are in reality "thick": many of our loves are acquired unintentionally through everyday practices which we take for granted.[25]

This is where Smith raises the concept of "liturgy" in an innovative way. He writes, "I want to ramp this up just one more notch and suggest that our thickest practices constitute and function as *liturgies*."[26] While we tend to think of liturgies in terms of religious practice, Smith says that "some so-called secular rituals actually constitute liturgies". He defines liturgies as "species of practice" or "rituals of ultimate concern" which are "formative for identity", "inculcate particular visions of the good life", and "do so in a way that means to trump other ritual formations."[27] For Smith, the use of the term 'liturgy' is important because it raises the stakes of what is taking place in our cultural practices and rituals.

This is where an understanding of how some of our cultural institutions operate is important (what Smith terms cultural exegesis) since cultural institutions are those conglomerations of practices (and built environment) that have unfolded and developed over time to address human needs, wants and desires.[28]

Furthermore, and pertinent to our "where-to-from-here", "understanding cultural institutions as liturgical institutions, as dynamic structures of desire, primes us to have a more heightened and nuanced appreciation of what's at stake in those institutions."[29]

So let's take some of Smith's cultural exegesis and the questions he poses, couple that with some of the conclusions arrived at in Chapters 2 and 3, and apply it to a suburban coastal context.

This cultural exegesis of our secular rituals and practices involves asking,

24. Smith, *Desiring the Kingdom*, 83.

25. Smith, *Desiring the Kingdom*, 85.

26. Smith, *Desiring the Kingdom*, 85.

27. Smith, *Desiring the Kingdom*, 86.

28. Smith, *Desiring the Kingdom*, 71.

29. Smith, *Desiring the Kingdom*, 73.

What vision of human flourishing is implicit in this or that practice? What does the good life look like as embedded in cultural
rituals? What sort of person will I become after being immersed in
this or that cultural liturgy?[30]

So 'secular liturgies' show that the so-called secular still testifies to
our religious nature, not just because it involves beliefs or "spiritual" mes-
sages, but because even the secular is eventually about love of something
ultimate.[31]

Therefore, in using some of Smith's framework coupled with our research, the remainder of this chapter will explore some of the secular liturgies and ascertain some points of contact, where we're able to show how
"disordered loves" can be reordered as we speak the gospel into particular
situations and even institutions. There remains a moment of affirmation, a
point of what Smith calls "apologetic contact."[32] Because there is an element
of these secular liturgies that can be built upon in our witness and mission,
we will explore a couple of examples of these now in the hope of providing
a small but synthesized roadmap for churches.

The liturgy of the surf

The conversations with pastors and community members show us clearly
that there is a deeply embedded cultural liturgy when it comes to beach
and surf micro-culture. "Where else would you rather be?" was the mantra
of the President of Cronulla Surf Life Saving Club. Often signing off his
President reports in the weekly newsletter to Club members, it defines a
liturgy attached to the beach and its micro-culture that perhaps not many
understand. As you make your way down the path through Cronulla Park
and see the sun sparkling off the water it's like you are being transported
somewhere else. People gather all over the esplanade from joggers to walk-
ers or those getting ready for their daily swim around Shark Island to those
perching for a coffee and just soaking in the environment, there's always an
energy but there is also a feel of calm and (perhaps) purpose.

The liturgy of the surf is defined by those with designated authority—the paid Council lifeguards or during the summer months the weekend volunteer Surf Life Savers who draw out the boundaries for those who

30. Smith, *Desiring the Kingdom*, 89.

31. Smith, *Desiring the Kingdom*, 122.

32. Smith, *Desiring the Kingdom*, 122.

would enter into the water. One settles on a spot either on the sand (if you want to sunbathe) or just on the large steps above the sand for those swimming around Shark Island or just out to the buoys.

There's a soothing, calming, almost cleansing aspect to the surf as you let the waves wash over you and you push off the bottom, punching through the surging, plunging walls of water rolling in. And as you survey the landscape and reflect upon the lifestyle, one is experiencing the good life.

This speaks directly into some of the conclusions I want to make as I draw various threads together. One such attempt is to shape an alternative narrative around this idea of the good life and the cultural liturgy of suburban coastal culture.

The liturgy of community

One of the themes that was picked up across a number of interviews was the desire people have for community. It is no secret that community is something people's hearts deeply desire, and they intentionally take steps to seek it out. Whether in a local café or in the park, local markets or different clubs, people are drawn to this sense of community and the good life that goes with it. So strong is the desire and longing that, as Kreminski points out, the strength of it means that people end up structuring their lives around this longing.[33]

In the late 20th century social researcher Hugh Mackay noted that "the story of Australia . . . has been a story of declining emphasis on personal relationships; less importance being attached to being a part of a family, a neighbourhood, a community; declining awareness of *shared* culture."[34] That was the later part of the 20th century. The truth is even more stark now. A perfect storm of cultural, sociological and even technological factors have fractured our social cohesion. However, as was the case then, so it is now that there still remains a desire to foster community within Australian culture. We see the strength of community in social clubs, sporting clubs and even as was gleaned from some interviews, communities within the wider suburban communities centering on other interests like food, music and coffee.

It comes as no surprise that as humans who are created in God's image as relational beings, we need one another to survive. In his book *Beyond*

33. Kreminski, *Urban Spirituality*, 41.

34. Mackay, *Reinventing Australia*, 54.

Belief, Mackay notes that there is great power that humans derive from their tribes, stemming from that deep need to connect. That is why we congregate and cooperate. It is of great importance, he says, that we establish and maintain the communities that sustain us.[35] In exploring the different forms that modern tribes take from schools to professional 'conferences', from tribes based on shared tastes or convictions to "a shared inclusion to hang out in certain places", he points to religion as "one of history's most obvious examples of how we satisfy our tribal yearnings."[36]

It is striking that just as church can offer a strong community of well-meaning and like-minded people, the church doesn't have a monopoly on these ideas. Community hubs like Surf Life Saving Clubs or even as Mackay points out, tribes sharing a similar conviction, can have a powerful pull. The question then becomes, what does the church have to offer that outweighs those factors whilst still fostering an authentic community? Mackay suggests that while in our more urbanised and sophisticated contexts churches are seen to not be as integral to the life of the community, the sense of the church as a community hub is still strong.[37] Citing the work of a property developer in Melbourne writing for the Victorian Planning Environmental Law Association, Rory Costelloe notes, "the important role that churches played historically in the development of social cohesion in the local community . . . the decline of this role has contributed to the increasing problem of alienation . . . from the neighbourhoods we live in."[38]

Juxtaposed with the deep desire for community is the problem of how to deal with the issues of loneliness and disconnection that are all-too prevalent. It is into these areas that churches can take concrete steps to be that "faithful presence". Kreminski sees solid concentrations of people in particular areas as being great opportunities to work with God's Spirit as a way of building authentic community.[39] In line with this, but perhaps with a slightly different nuance, churches would do well to consider their already developed communities and look at how God's people can speak into those.

When asked what he saw as being the place of the church within the community, one figure described it to the author as a community, or in the case of the many churches located within a small proximity to one

35. Mackay, *Beyond Belief,* 35.

36. Mackay, *Beyond Belief,* 36.

37. Mackay, *Beyond Belief,* 55.

38. Mackay, *Beyond Belief,* 55.

39. Kreminski, *Urban Spirituality,* 42.

another in Cronulla, "communities within the community". The same, he suggested, could be said of an institution like the Surf Club and of course we could extend this to any organisation that sees the same group of people gathering on a regular basis with a common purpose. This is because the whole idea of community conveys a certain set of common values such as connectivity, respect, care and interdependence.[40] It is true for Surf Clubs, churches, RSL clubs and sports clubs. But deep down as God's people we know the church on mission, making disciples, holds out that true sense of belonging. There is a sense of lostness, drifting and even disconnection when we don't feel like we belong. It is no wonder then, that "part of our identity comes from our connection and relationship with others so when we lose it, it can be very disorienting."[41]

This is because as humans we're made in God's image who is himself God in community, or theologically speaking, Trinitarian. This means that community, not individualism, is at the core of what it means to be human. Kreminiski identifies this as important for urban spirituality, "which highlights relationship and community as opposed to individualism and isolation."[42]

If the doctrine of the Trinity leads us to see that life in its essence is about relationships, it follows that true Trinitarian community would be crucial for Christians to embody in a world sadly littered with people who experience loneliness, fragmentation and alienation.[43] Churches are communities by virtue of what it means to be the people of God (for example, the 'one another' phrases littered throughout the New Testament letters show us this). Kreminski believes that the church must itself display a deeper expression of community in our world as a witness. We have an opportunity to counter the false narratives of our world, such as Bonhoeffer offers about the place of community in his book *Life Together*, as we seek to show a practiced and embodied love towards others.[44] But as much as we might feel like it, often there's much the church can learn from other groups about what community looks like.

Clearly the churches which have connected well are able to see the yearning people have for community in their suburbs. They are developing

40. Kreminski, *Urban Spirituality*, 40-41.

41. Kreminski, *Urban Spirituality*, 41.

42. Kreminski, *Urban Spirituality*, 48.

43. Kreminski, *Urban Spirituality*, 49.

44. Bonhoeffer, *Life Together*, 23.

a model of ministry that looks at people's longings and hopes and then shows how the gospel or a Christian worldview can speak powerfully into that.

My research has pointed to desires on the part of most, if not all, ministers to engage in a meaningful way with their communities which suggests an underlying missional desire to point people towards the beauty and truth of the gospel. For example, two churches which were interviewed haven't tried to compete with the established community of the Surf Life Saving Nippers movement, but people from within the church have joined this particular local community hub.[45] Interestingly the church, recognising the already-established reach that Nippers has historically, had at one of their locations, structured their Sunday services around Nippers so as to not compete with them. They provided church at a time where both their people can be a faithful presence within that movement and then have a church service to which they can invite those whose lives are already deeply enmeshed within the Surf Life Saving/Nippers culture.

Kreminski believes that how we think about community is crucial for a description of urban spirituality, but this most definitely applies to the suburban as well, since people today long for community and long for places that foster strong relationships.[46] Interestingly, Hugh Mackay has also noticed this, saying:

> If you are ever tempted by the thought that contemporary Western culture is more individualistic than in the past just take a look around you. From the family to the workplace, from the school gate to the local coffee shop or pub, and from religious, political or sporting affiliations to friendship circles, both online and offline, we are as socially interdependent as ever. Our default position as humans is together even for those of us who cherish time alone.[47]

It is my conviction that the model for ecclesiology and missiology steeped in the atonement can then provide a picture of what Christian community looks like and has much to contribute in a culture of yearnings for belonging in the midst of dislocation and loneliness. Having engaged with

---

45. It's worth pointing out that members of one of these churches located on one of Sydney's most famous beaches have joined other local community hubs recognising the importance of having that faithful presence in other significant community organisations: in their case the local municipal council is another good example.

46. Kreminski, *Urban Spirituality*, 80.

47. Mackay, *What Makes us Tick*, 51.

the culture and carried out the necessary contextualisation in identifying those secular liturgies and showing how the gospel provides a better way, churches are in a position to create spaces for community and relationships "where people who are different can embrace one another."[48] This is where the nexus of the atonement model for the church to operate in its ecclesiology and missiology comes into play in creating that "Third Place". I established in chapter 2 how the atonement provides us with a framework for attaching Third Places to the church, thus providing a place of belonging and community. Three of the church leaders interviewed have tried intentionally to create a community space within their church, with different degrees of success.

For Stuart Crawshaw, the atonement approach means that as the Cross is preached within the gathering showing people God's mercy, there is incorporated into the gathering of God's people a "Third Place" community. At this particular Anglican church plant in the Sutherland Shire, as the Senior Pastor, Stuart has overseen the incorporation of meals as well as a strong sense of belonging into their fellowship together.

As they embrace hospitality and friendship, he says:

> As we learn to be friends with those who we live next to instead of those we like because of common interests and values, this challenges the status quo and transforms us in ways we might not have expected.[49]

This wholistic approach to Christian community counters some of those false cultural narratives with practices that speak directly into people's longings and hopes while at the same time showing people what authentic community and true discipleship looks like. As Newbigin puts it,

> I have come to feel that the primary reality of which we have to take account in seeking for a Christian impact on public life is the Christian congregation . . . [Jesus] did not write a book but formed a community.[50]

This is a helpful link to the previous discussion surrounding the "Nones". Gene Veith points out that one thing sometimes lacking for the "Nones", though they have their 'religious' practices, is that they do not participate in any kind of religious community. They don't even go to

---

48. Crawshaw, Recorded Interview, 2020.

49. Crawshaw, Recorded Interview, 2020.

50. Newbigin, *Pluralist Society*, 227.

Spiritualist or New Age groups despite their spirituality mantra.[51] With little community apart perhaps from the online, it makes sense then that establishing a "Third Place" community in the life of the church that emphasizes some aspects of church life which would speak into the desires of the "Nones" community is a powerful thing. Community can be (re)built through the preaching of the gospel coupled with a discipline of hospitality and friendship which may help reorient the "Nones". In these post-Christian times, the task becomes to establish a church that re-embraces community, and, in a world where 'spiritual' and "religious" are viewed as opposite categories, put these categories back together.

Fostering a "Faithful Presence"

Third and finally, it is my hope that as churches embrace the challenge of an urban spirituality and discover a deeper understanding of their particular micro-cultures and what drives them, this will place them in a good position to pursue the common good and seek the wellbeing of the suburb by embracing that notion of being a "faithful presence". This, according to James Davison Hunter, "is in keeping with the instruction that the people of God are to be committed to the welfare of the cities in which they reside in exile, even when the city is indifferent, hostile or ungrateful."[52]

This isn't necessarily a new notion but rather an older wisdom. However as we live out these truths we are embodying real community because notice where the mission takes place: in the neighbourhood, in the workplace, in the home—not in the meetings of the church. We reach a hostile world by living good lives in the context of ordinary life: showing people the real difference Jesus makes in the context of everyday mission. And in doing so we work with God to bring the message of the salvation, peace, justice, mercy and love that come through him into the community.

My research provided us with a picture of a missional element in ministers' thinking: the churches that have sought to/are seeking to embrace that faithful presence, is attested by their examples of being good neighbours or guests of local community hubs. From fostering a faithful presence in the school community through working bees or providing other services, to people in the church joining the local Surf Club and even being trained as Chaplains for the purpose of embracing those in

51. Veith, *Post Christian*, 240.
52. Hunter, *Change the World*, 278.

those communities. These can have a deep and lasting impact upon these coastal contexts as the church becomes a gospel community with a missional focus—serving its neighbourhood together.

Truly Missional

In much of the literature that we come across, the word "missional" is used in many and diverse ways. I showed in Chapter 3 that the best way to think about being missional is to look at it from what we know about the God who is the God of mission.

Being 'missional' isn't just about doing more outreach activities or even doing those for the sake of having outreach.[53] Indeed we have already used the biblical narrative of God's work of redemption throughout history to define God's mission (highlighting God's mission to redeem and restore his blessing on all humanity). "This is the mission of God: to restore the creation and the life of humanity from the ravages of sin."[54]

The missional church, representing the Kingdom, requires an outward focus beyond the life of the church. If a church is outward focused, it is engaged in mission in its community with people outside of the faith. We have seen how Guder and others provide clear biblical evidence that God calls the church to take the gospel of Jesus Christ to its own community.

As the sent people of God, "missional" is also about our identity as Christians, or as Kreminiski puts it, "to be missional is to understand that our deepest identity is that we are children of God sent into the world to cooperate with the mission of God."[55] Thus, also in a sense, God's people as the church embody the gospel by designing practices that are missional: practices which engage on a real level with our culture.

The church must have an outward focus to accomplish this mission. However this ought not happen at the expense of the church being the church. Indeed it is my contention that the abandonment of institutional church for more cutting-edge "fresh" expressions doesn't necessarily provide the answer.

Christians certainly must consider how to be incarnational. Frost and Hirsch are right to point out that Jesus' incarnation can provide a way of seeing our missional task in the world in that it helps us understand our mission

53. Kreminski, *Urban Spirituality*, 31.

54. Goheen, *Light to the Nations*, 19.

55. Kreminski, *Urban Spirituality*, 31.

as we "move into the neighbourhood" in the direction of those who are spiritually lost.[56] While there is much to commend in the missional edge of those driven by an incarnational theology and the desire to push the church in its thinking outside the bounds of our Christendom mindset, the church (as I established in Chapter 2) must retain its identity. There is something good and beautiful about the ordinary grace-infused communal liturgy of the church that can point people to the Creator who is the only one who by his Spirit re-orients and reorders our "disordered loves".[57]

Let me repeat: we need to go where people are, rather than expecting them to come to us which harkens back to the old Christendom model. For Kreminski, rather than creating a fresh expression of church which to some nearly abandons church heritage, going to where people are in shared spaces is a way of discerning "what God is already doing as a lead-in to being able to connect, serve and bless our community."[58] Her incarnational spirituality encourages us to love our neighbourhoods by praying for our areas, being good neighbours and practicing stability and faithfulness where we are, which "can yield relationships grounded in trust, which can bring the right people to speak into people's lives at appropriate moments."[59]

This is where the notion of the church as a "Third Place" from our discussion in Chapter 4 still has merit. The beaches are fashionable and fun places to visit. Suburbs like Cronulla are now highly sought-after places in which to live and raise a family. Thus as William McAlpine puts it, "Place is more than location; it is a meaningful interaction of activity and persons within location."[60]

The church can be that place as an authentic community within communities. In doing so it does what Kreminski, Smith, Sayers and others have attempted to do: recover an authentic Christianity in an attempt to shift away from the sacred/secular divide that has permeated many attempts to bridge gaps and work out just how to engage with culture and embody God's love in our contexts.

If the world and all in it belong to God, there can be no sphere of life that is not open to his rule. This was the attempt of the "Christ against Culture" proponents who sought to chart a way forward. But as we have

56. Frost and Hirsch, *Shaping of Things*, 35.

57. Smith, *Awaiting the King*, 76.

58. Kreminski, *Urban Spirituality*, 35.

59. Kreminski, *Urban Spirituality*, 85.

60. McAlpine, *Sacred Space for the Missional Church*, quoted in Kreminski, 65.

seen with Kreminski's model of urban spirituality, Smith's push for us to develop a sustained exegesis of cultural liturgies and the way that allows us to work towards helping people reorient their "disordered loves", and Sayers' penetrating cultural analysis show how historically we may have unwittingly bought into the Gnostic dualistic approach.

And so, as we begin to combine all spheres of life under the rule of God, we are committing all our lives under Jesus, meaning God's people are able to live well showing the truth of Jesus, the beauty of Christian community and the liveability of the gospel that impacts every area of life. When we put Jesus front and centre, confessing him as Lord, we take seriously the absolute and ongoing centrality of Jesus for Christianity as a movement and for the local gathering."[61] It's obvious that we must keep Jesus front and centre, for he is the one who changes everything by virtue of his sin-bearing death, resurrection to new life and exaltation to God's right hand as Lord of all.

Out of the many practices suggested by Hirsch in his *Forgotten Ways Handbook*, the one pertinent to this discussion is shaping life and spirituality on Jesus. This means assessing what we do and modelling a spirituality of engagement with our world that embraces a ministry of faithful presence. One key factor is having that sustained active presence in the community and a good understanding of the community in which we find ourselves. Of the churches researched, it is clear that ministers who take or are taking a long-term view of ministry in these suburbs are able to develop (alongside their staff teams and other lay leaders) a solid ministry of presence in their community. This is particularly so for those churches that identified the spheres of influence (such as the Surf Lifesaving Club), and then were able to become members of those clubs and develop authentic caring relationships. The role of Community Chaplains (in this case sports chaplains—but there is scope for the reach to be wider) and creating links with the local church cannot be underestimated.

An approach like this is a way in which we are able to ask people to join with us, as we live out and embody God's rule where the atonement is the basis for all that is done. Church becomes not just a gathering place but where God's people are taught and nurtured in such a way that disciples are made and as Romans 12 is lived out, mission is infused into the culture—it becomes a way of life. This is where discipleship and training come in.

---

61. Hirsch, *Forgotten Ways Handbook*, 42.

A More Intentional Discipleship

Discipleship is a key theme of Matthew's Gospel and its importance is seen no more so than in The Great Commission.

Not limited just to the Twelve, disciples are those who follow after (*akolouthein*) Jesus. They are the blessed ones (5:11), the children of God, and they are modelled on Jesus himself.[62] And while they're held up as "ideals to emulate" it's also clear that the picture painted of them is not by any means embellished as is evidenced by Matthew's comment prior to the Great Commission that, "When they saw him they worshipped him but some doubted" (Matt 28:17). In fact, as Bosch points out, Matthew could well be looking at the members of the community to which he writes, in their experience of difficulty in defining their own identity so as to remind them "of a rather bewildered band of simple folk on the slopes of a mountain in Galilee."[63] In this moment of doubt and weakness for these disciples, the announcement of Jesus' Lordship is inextricably linked with the challenge to make and to be disciples, for "being a disciple means living out the teachings of Jesus."[64]

As the church carries out God's mission, articulated by Jesus in the Great Commission, at its core will be the desire to make "disciple-making disciples". This is obviously important for the growth of God's church and the glory of his Kingdom. However, this hasn't always been the case. This book has already established that the church in Australia (and particularly the Reformed Evangelical scene) has struggled not just because we find ourselves living in a "skeptical world", but because we have been stuck on the model of Christendom, which placed the church at the centre of the culture. In the culture of Christendom, the church's mission was to meet the needs of its members. This led to an inherently inward focus. The church became absorbed with its own hierarchy and organisation. Indeed, as Alan Hirsch points out, Christendom has developed over a long period of time recognised professional clergy acting primarily in the pastor/service provider mode. While it's the case that the majority of churches whose ministers I interviewed had long since moved past this model, we perceived there is still a struggle for some churches to energise and mobilise their people for mission.

---

62. Bosch, *Transforming Mission*, 76.

63. Bosch, *Transforming Mission*, 78.

64. Bosch, *Transforming Mission*, 82.

Despite the struggle, there is clearly a deep desire on the part of ministers to see people discipled well through small groups and equipped for mission by creating a culture of mission within the church.

The driving force behind this, over the last ten years, stems from the publication of *The Trellis and the Vine* which promoted seismic shifts in the way churches shaped their approach to ministry. Shifting from a programmatic emphasis to a relational approach, ministry was defined no longer by the number of programs but by the extent and quality of relationships. It marked a shift from a marketing approach to a discipleship and training model.

Payne and Marshall argue that, in order to institute a culture of disciple-making, there needed to be a shift from clergy being seen as service providers, to big-picture thinkers and also trainers and equippers.[65] Indeed, this kind of ministry shift encouraged everyone to see themselves as a disciple-making disciple which in turn recaptures one of the essential factors of the Protestant Reformation: the priesthood of all believers. Keller contends that this will mean every believer, amongst other important facets of church life, will have the priestly calling to "do good and share with others." (Heb 13:16)[66] This makes the shared, gift-shaped ministry of all members a key element of the outward focused, missional church.[67]

Equipping God's people with a clear understanding of the Kingdom of God and the true nature of God's mission helps them to understand the urgency of the task as well as the importance of an outward community focus, rather than a narrow, inward view of the church as an organisation. If our "citizenship is in heaven, and from it we eagerly await a Saviour, the Lord Jesus Christ" (Phil 3:20), then living faithfully to that allegiance becomes a calling every day and is not limited to activities in church.

Therefore, the church must take a fresh look at the community. My research has shown the importance of pastors modelling a cultural exegesis to their congregations. "God's people must communicate the truthful reality of God's message to persons living within particular cultural contexts. This task makes it imperative that God's people understand the culture within which they live and minister".[68] In the words of the apostle

---

65. Payne and Marshall, *Trellis and the Vine*, 34.

66. Keller, *Center Church*, 345.

67. Van Gelder, *Missional Church*, 58.

68. Hunsberger and Van Gelder, *Church Between*, 53.

Paul, we seek to "become all things to all people that by all means I might save some." (1 Cor 9:22)

As churches disciple their members in this way, helping them adapt to changes in the culture, there are other aspects worth keeping in mind. In our post-Christendom situation, inviting people to worship is inadequate and ineffective by itself. Yet, this is what many Christians have been urged to do. This is all that they know. Therefore, given the social and cultural changes in our society, the ongoing challenge lies in equipping believers to be on mission *in the everyday*, by discipling and equipping God's people in how to articulate the gospel clearly, how to share their story of how God has transformed them, and how to address questions and objections. One pastor put it to us this way as they have sought to build,

> . . . those strengths around that kind of a twin focus around evangelism and discipleship and what does it look like to equip people well in order to reach out into their families, businesses in that kind of environment . . . what does it look like for people to think that they're on mission in their street or their neighbourhood or their workplace, family, those things. But we've seen [the] fruit of that, that people kind of recognise those opportunities, and then we'd sort of equip in different ways with different ways that we might train [them] up.

In doing so they have deliberately steered away from that attractional mode and instead have tried to encourage people to take their faith into those places. Crosweller articulates it in this way:

> We need much more to recover a vision for evangelism where the load carried is as light as the gospel message, and feet can move swiftly because they are not keeping step with a congregational crowd. Where this happens, there is a simplicity to evangelism. After all, you have little present but a person and the evangel! There we can be confident of a trust in the evangel as the means of mission, for there is simply nothing else there to put the trust in! Such evangelism nourishes the church.[69]

Thus, discipling church members, training them to understand their context and then releasing them into their contexts to be that faithful presence should be part of the overall goal.

Furthermore, it is also important to recognise that some methods of evangelism were developed for a different cultural context, in which a

---

69. Crosweller, "This is This," lines 73-76.

WHERE DO WE GO FROM HERE?

majority of people either recognised the authority of Scripture or were acquainted with some of the central narratives of the Bible. This is no longer the case and so in this post-Christian context, evangelism must involve building relationships so that we can understand the background and questions of each person. Without the opportunity to hear each person's individual story we run the risk of ignoring their misconceptions of the gospel and of Jesus Christ. Thus, stereotypes of evangelism are only strengthened in the unchurched person's mind. No one wants to feel that they are a mission object. How can the non-Christian have the opportunity to understand Christianity as a way of life unless Christians are engaged in their community and are building relationships within their spheres of influence?

Tim Foster's *Suburban Captivity of the Church* provides a helpful framework for addressing this issue, where he differentiates between a "punitive" and a "telic" gospel. The punitive gospel focuses on trying to establish a certain set of categories that help people 'know' the truth, and with a particular (almost exclusive) emphasis on penal substitutionary atonement and its individual implications as the "entire" gospel. This isn't wrong, but it is *limited* in its scope. His telic gospel approach provides a big picture understanding that humanity in their rebellion against God (sin) have undermined and broken the world God created. But in the atonement, Jesus deals with the problem, penalty and power of our sin. His resurrection from the dead, defeating death, points to a new future and a new reality that in one sense has already begun. Christians are therefore called to live in the light of this new reality, working with God on his mission in our world such that "the Christian life, sometimes called discipleship, flows naturally from the gospel: the new order in which Jesus is Lord."[70]

Our aim must be then to continue to ensure that the people in churches can see clearly how the gospel impacts the whole of life so as to avoid the disconnect between what we believe and living that out. As we embody God's mission by being that faithful presence in our spheres of influence, we want to equip people to speak the gospel in its fullness to their neighbours, friends and workmates in ways that resonate with their hearts. We want to be able to, as Sam Chan models in his book *Evangelism in a Skeptical World*, connect the stories of the Gospels (and indeed the bigger story of God's reign) to people's stories so that they might, as Kreminski puts it, "give up their lesser and destructive cultural narratives and join with us in

---

70. Foster, *Suburban Captivity*, 24-25.

the Story that we seek to live ou.t.[71] Perhaps in one sense leaders need to re-evangelise their flock. This is a task of positive persuasion, for we have a better story of good news we need to tell.

Clearly a very intentional and a significant focus on making disciples of Jesus Christ and equipping people for participation in mission has been and is important for the life of the church as it seeks to reach various micro-cultures. We live in a culture dominated by non-Christian thought and themes (about reason/science, individualism, relativism, materialism). Therefore, it is worth churches pouring time into training and equipping their people to help them think about what it looks like to be a faithful presence in their local club or their neighbourhood or their workplace, and even in their families by integrating their faith into these spheres. The onus is on our churches to provide the means whereby they can train and disciple their members. In an article (based on his book of the same name) entitled *How to Reach the West (Again)*, Tim Keller suggests that when Christians are equipped to do this,

> . . . the gospel will become 'salt and light' in culture more naturally than if we take a more *political* approach in which Christians seek to gain the reins of coercive power, or take a more *withdrawn* approach in which being a Christian is seen as something you only do in private with no application to every area of life.[72]

Thus, where training in evangelism and discipleship is happening intentionally and being modelled, my research showed there is fruit being borne. We have learned that the importance cannot be underestimated for churches recognising and taking those opportunities to equip their people in different ways, in their thinking and praxis around evangelism, in moving their attention from the church to the neighbourhood and being that faithful presence so that they might become missionaries in their communities. Practically speaking, here are some very brief suggestions on what this could look like in these semi-urban/suburban coastal contexts. It is our hope that these principles would translate into other contexts with particular micro-cultures.

We have also seen that where leaders build into their church's DNA a culture of training in evangelism and discipleship that equips people to lean out into their communities courageously to be that faithful missionary

71. Kreminski, *Urban Spirituality*, 100.

72. Keller, "Reach the West," 2020

presence in the everyday, it paves the way to have a more intentional missional focus. For example, it might mean encouraging young mums from church to work out those rhythms or times when other young mums from the suburb are gathering at the local parks. It could mean following the examples of the churches whose ministers I interviewed who have become that faithful presence in their local schools by offering practical volunteer help with working bees or being around for open days.

To help you think about other ways forward for your church in a suburban coastal context, let me finish with the example of one particular church to show how this could be done in plenty of other contexts. Over the course of a few years, one Church established a faithful presence within the local SLSC by way of the involvement of their Assistant Minister and some other church members. This presence has meant that at the start of the Surf Life Saving season, the church, in partnership with the two Surf Life Saving Clubs, held a "Preseason Blessing" at the local Anglican Church attended by various members of the Surf Clubs. The service was led by the church's Assistant Minister. The Club's President also attended, along with a local government minister and the Surf Club Chaplain. Visitors received a message on how Jesus is both the Servant and Saviour, and the service included a time of prayer for the upcoming season. Some guests even took a copy of the Lifesaving Bible home with them.

It is worth also stating that there are many, many more ways this can be enacted according to each church's community and situation. The principles and ways forward I have suggested here aren't necessarily limited to churches in beachside suburbs, and in the end they need only be limited by the creativity of each church in their own contexts.

Conclusion

Despite our marginalisation and the fact that churches in this post-Christian context are very much in a situation of exile, we have something to offer our coastal contexts, and we have something to offer the spiritual but non-religious. We can still make an impact, but we need to think differently. It is vitally important to equip people in our churches to embrace exile and think about church life together as being "on mission" in the ordinariness of everyday life. We need to continue to think through what it would look like to move beyond church as just a weekly service, to a community that shares life and mission. Can we be a people for whom church and mission are our identity rather than occasional events?[1]

The people of God living life together on mission *is* the good life: we are made for community with God and others. We therefore want to teach and train our people and release them to be a gospel community, doing good, and bringing blessing to those around them. It is the good life and works of the church community and its life in the face of an apathetic, strongly hedonistic culture that will provoke questions about what we put our hope in and what we build our identity around. It is through exposure to the community of grace that people start to see that followers of Jesus are energised by their desire to work together to witness to Christ in their context.

As disciples of the Lord Jesus have their concern for the lost re-energised, this expression will take different forms in different church contexts for different people. It would be wonderful to see some believers gain the confidence and competence to train in sports chaplaincy and equipped to be a faithful presence in their local sports club. It is hoped others might be

1. Timmis and Chester, *Everyday Church*, 154.

174

encouraged to engage with friends or work colleagues in their spheres of influence, with the gospel of Jesus Christ. The reality is in a sinful and post-Christian era, this process requires training and equipping embedded in the cultural DNA of churches if it is to be realistic and effective.

As this happens, it is my deep desire that churches in these coastal contexts (and this could apply beyond the Sydney Metropolitan area) can be encouraged to explore further ways in which they're able to focus on reorienting people's disordered loves. This can be achieved, in part, through a deeper understanding of secular liturgies by way of cultural exegesis as we seek to show how people's secular liturgies or notions of community and the good life are met in and answered by the God of creation who has revealed himself in the Scriptures. Further, it is the belief of the author that it is worth encouraging churches to consider how adopting a "Third Place" model of ministry, founded on the atonement, could enable them to reconnect with the micro-cultures of their contexts by building a solid community of Christians devoted to service and sacrifice.

Moreover, as I have learnt from the range of interviews and indeed from interacting with other literature, practicing an urban spirituality as well as fostering a faithful presence through discipleship can have an impact upon our communities, allowing churches to become significant communities within their community. In moving our attention from the church to these communities and micro-cultures, we join God on his mission in those spaces. It is most certainly a slow work, but it means beginning to look at certain places that hold special meaning and carry local significance in our local community. For many of these places are seen as sacred to the locals in a particular context.[2] It is therefore up to us to understand and engage with the cultural liturgies of those places as we engage with God's redemptive activity in his world.

In the end, our desire must be for the church to be what God has called it to be—a visible witness in our local communities that asks people to join with us as we embody what it looks to be the chosen and saved people of God on mission together. How wonderful it would be to see churches in these areas, and beyond, proclaiming and promoting in word and deed the glorious gospel of the risen Lord Jesus—the gospel which captures the hearts and minds of people to win the lost, so that many in these coastal contexts throughout Sydney and even beyond might be won for the Lord Jesus Christ.

---

2. Kreminski, *Urban Spirituality*, 125.

Appendix 1

Invitation to Participate in Interview

Letter

Dear [pastor of selected church],

I am writing to invite you take part in an interview as a minister who is an incumbent in a beachside parish in the Sydney Diocese.

The purpose of these interviews is to give me the opportunity to draw alongside church incumbents like yourself to see 'what's happening and what are the main challenges that incumbents face in parish ministry located in beachside suburbs in Sydney.

I am currently enrolled in the Doctor of Ministry program at Trinity Evangelical Divinity School, (Deerfield Illinois). I am about to commence a research project that intends to explore the challenges for ministry and growth in churches located in beachside suburbs in Sydney and the Northern Illawarra. Hence, I am looking for rectors, or curates-in-charge who would be interested in and willing to participate in the research by sharing their experiences. The involvement will not be onerous, just one interview with me. At the outset please be assured that the interviews will be conducted in complete confidence and will follow the strict ethical guidelines set down by the Human Rights in Research (HRR) protocol.

I would like to invite you to participate in this research, and I look forward to hearing from you at your earliest convenience. I will follow this letter up with a phone call in the next two weeks.

Yours in the partnership of the Gospel,

Rev. Richard Wenden

Appendix 2

Consent for Participation in Interview Research

I VOLUNTEER TO PARTICIPATE in an interview conducted by Richard Wenden from St Andrew's Anglican Church Cronulla as part of a research project for the Doctor of Ministry Program at Trinity Evangelical Divinity School. I understand that the project is designed to gather information about my locality, social trends and religious background.

1. My participation in this project is voluntary. I understand that I will not be paid for my participation. I may withdraw and discontinue participation at any time without penalty.

2. I understand that most interviewees will find the discussion interesting and thought-provoking. If, however, I feel uncomfortable in any way during the interview session, I have the right to decline to answer any question or to end the interview.

3. The interview will last approximately 45-90 minutes. Notes will be written during the interview. The interview will be recorded. If I don't want to be taped, I will not be able to participate in the study.

4. I understand that the researcher will not identify me by name in any reports using information obtained from this interview, and that my confidentiality as a participant in this study will remain secure. Subsequent uses of records and data will be subject to standard data use

policies which protect the anonymity of individuals and institutions. Recordings will be destroyed on completion of the project.

5. I understand that this research study has been reviewed and approved by the Human Rights in Research Committee at Trinity Evangelical Divinity School.

6. I have read and understand the explanation provided to me. I have had all my questions answered to my satisfaction, and I voluntarily agree to participate in this study.

7. I have been given a copy of this consent form.

_____ My Signature

_____ My Printed Name

For further information, please contact:

Rev. Richard Wenden
1a St Andrew's Place
CRONULLA NSW 2230
rector@cronulla.anglican.asn.au
0410 546 682

Appendix 3

Survey & Interview Questions for Ministers

1. How long have you served at your church?

   - 0-5 years
   - 6-10 years
   - 10-15 years
   - 16-20 years

2. What are the top 5 strengths of your church's ministry?

   -
   -
   -
   -
   -

3. What are the 5 biggest needs/challenges your church faces in your context?

   -
   -

-
-
-

4. Tell me about your outreach activities, how many times a week would you be engaged in outreach?

    - Never
    - 1-2 times a month
    - 1-2 times a week
    - 3-5 times a week
    - 6-7 times a week
    - More _____

5. How often are your staff members engaged in formal church outreach activities

6. What efforts have you made to understand your community in the time you've been here and how well do you now think you understand your community?

7. How well do you think your congregation is able to engage outsiders with the gospel?

8. In the time you have served as Senior Pastor, how well do you think your church has engaged in the past with the suburb?

One of the influencing factors when it comes to church attendance is the myriad of other activities/communities people choose to be a part of. The focus of this research is on the impact of participation that Surf Life Saving activities has when it comes to church attendance. The next block of questions focuses on this:

9. How many of your families would be involved with Surf Life Saving Nippers in the Surf Life Saving Season

10. How do you go about encouraging church families who are involved in Nippers to continue intentionally meeting with other Christians?

    (Prompt: either at church or some other gathering)

11. What specific strategies has your church tried to reach the SLS Nipper community and what has been their effectiveness?

12. Does the Surf Life Saving club in your Parish have a chaplain attached to it?

- Yes
  i. P/T
  ii. F/T
- No
- Pending

I'd like to know something about their role in the club:

   a. To start with is the chaplain a member of your church?

   b. If yes, could you tell me how long they have served as chaplain?

- Tell me please about their ministry?
- Which of their strategies, approaches etc., have worked particularly well/which strategies didn't work well?
- If the chaplain is not a member of your church how useful would it be to develop a link between surf life saving chaplaincy and the churches in your Parish (assuming there isn't one already)?
- What contextual factors or conditions appear to facilitate or impede the impact of their work in this role?

Appendix 4

Community Interview
Invitation Letter

Dear [member of community],

I am writing to invite you take part in an interview as someone who is a key stakeholder within our community.

The purpose of these interviews is to give me the opportunity see what's happening and get more of a feel for the culture and history of our area from your point of view as a long-term resident in the Shire. This is a helpful part of my research as I explore the main challenges that pastors face in parish ministry located in beachside suburbs in Sydney.

I am currently enrolled in the Doctor of Ministry program at Trinity Evangelical Divinity School, (Deerfield Illinois). The involvement will not be onerous, just one interview with me. At the outset please be assured that the interviews will be conducted in complete confidence and will follow the strict ethical guidelines set down by the Human Rights in Research (HRR) protocol.

I would like to invite you to participate in this research, and I look forward to hearing from you at your earliest convenience. I will follow this letter up with a phone call in the next two weeks.

Yours faithfully,

Rev. Richard Wenden

Appendix 5

Community 'Gatekeeper'
Interview Questions

1. Tell me about your experiences of life in this suburb?

    Having lived in Cronulla for 9 years, I've seen some changes; you have most likely seen significant change as well.

2. Tell me about the big changes you've seen over the past 10-20 years?

    (Prompt: significant cultural ones e.g., Sport, shopping, lifestyle)

    In your view what effect have these changes had on how people spend their time

    Now specifically, what activities do people tend to do on Sundays? (identifying how people spend their Sundays

3. Now think back to when you were growing up—what did you do on Sundays then?

4. Did your family go to church?

    a. If yes, tell me about your involvement in church growing up?

    b. If no, what can you recall—was it something that didn't interest your parents? Was there a particular reason why they didn't attend church?

5. What sort of Christian teaching (if any) did you have growing up and what effect, if any, did it have on you?

   Prompt: here are some examples

Scripture (SRE)	Holiday Camps
Sunday School	Church
School	Friends, family

6. The number of people attending church has declined over the years and part of my research is seeking to understand some of the reasons behind this.

   a. What sort of factors led to you dropping out of church?

   b. what factors in your opinion have contributed to this decline in attendance?

7. Thinking about the place of the church in the community today:

   a. In what areas do you see churches involved in the community these days?

   b. What could the church do to make itself more relevant in the eyes of the community?

8. Do you have any additional comments that you think would help me understand how our church fits into, is perceived by and the role it can continue to play in the community?

Bibliography

Achtemeier, Paul, J. 1996. *1 Peter: A Commentary on First Peter*. University of Michigan: Fortress.

Adam, Peter. 2006. *Incarnational Theology for a Missionary Church*. St Mark's Review 200, 14-21.

Ammerman, Nancy, Jackson Carroll, W., Carl Dudley, S., and William McKinney, eds. 1998. *Studying Congregations: A New Handbook*. South Nashville, TN: Abingdon Press.

Bailey, A, Carol. 2007. *A Guide to Qualitative Field Research*. 2nd ed. Thousand Oaks, CA: Pine Forge.

Bauckham, Richard. 2015. 'Reading Scripture as a Coherent Story', *The Bible in the Contemporary Word: Hermeneutical Ventures*. Grand Rapids, MI: Eerdmans.

Bonhoeffer, Dietrich. 1934. *Life Together*. New York, NY: HarperOne.

Bosch, David J. 1991. *Transforming Mission: Paradigm Shifts in Theology of Mission*. Maryknoll, NY: Orbis.

Boyley, Mark. 2004. "1 Peter – A Mission Document?" *The Reformed Theological Review*. 63 no.2 (August): 72-86.

Brueggemann, Walter. 1997. *Cadences of Home: Preaching Among Exiles*. Lousville, Westminster: John Knox.

Bryant, Nick. 'The Shire versus Australia: How a New Show is Creating Drama'. https://www.themonthly.com.au/issue/2012/june/1341970621/nick-bryant/shire-versus-australia#mtr.

Calvin, Jean. 1960. *Institutes of the Christian Religion*. Edited by John T. McNeill, and Ford Lewis Battles. 2 vols. Philadelphia, Pennsylvania: Westminster Press.

Cameron, Marcia. 2006. *An Enigmatic Life: David Broughton Knox, Father of Contemporary Sydney Anglicanism*. Brunswick East, Victoria: Acorn.

Chan, Sam. 2018. *Evangelism in a Skeptical World: How to Make the Unbelievable News about Jesus more Believable*. Grand Rapids, MI: Zondervan.

Clowney, Edmund, P. 1995. *The Church*. Contours of Christian Theology. Downers Grove, IL: Intervarsity Press.

Creswell, John W. 2014. *Research Design: Qualitative, Quantitative & Mixed Methods Approaches*. Los Angeles, CA: SAGE.

BIBLIOGRAPHY

Crosweller. 2016. 'This is This': Church, Evangelism (& Why they are not the same thing). Accessed January 21, 2019. https://stjohnsmaroubra.com/blog/2016/10/10/ymhl37aneuqbsosyooksm8r2nhnqek

Curby, Pauline. 1998. *A Pictorial History of Cronulla.* Crows Nest, NSW: Kingsclear Books.

Dever, Mark. 2007. *The Gospel and Personal Evangelism.* Wheaton, IL: Crossway.

Dickson, John P. 2003. *Mission-Commitment in Ancient Judaism and in the Pauline Communities: The Shape, Extent and Background of Early Christian Mission.* WUNT, 2/159; Tübingen: Mohr Siebeck.

Dickson, John, P. 2010. *The Best Kept Secret of Christian Mission.* Grand Rapids, MI: Zondervan.

Drake, H. A. 2004. *Constantine and the Bishops: The Politics of intolerance* quoted in Stuart Murray, *Post-Christendom: Church and Mission in a Strange New World* (Carlisle: Paternoster, 2004).

Drescher, Elizabeth. 2016. *Choosing Our Religion: The Spiritual Lives of America's Nones.* New York: Oxford University Press.

Edwards, Dennis R., Tremper Longman, and Scot McKnight. 2017. *1 Peter* Grand Rapids, Michigan: Zondervan.

Eliot, T. S. 1934. 'Choruses from the Rock' in Collected Poems 1909-1962, faber and faber.

Emery White, James. 2014. *The Rise of the Nones.* 1st ed. Grand Rapids, MI: Baker Academic.

Fagbemi, Stephen A. A. 2009. "Living for Christ in a hostile world: the Christian Identity and its Present Challenges in 1 Peter." *Transformation* 26 (1): 1-14.

Foster, Tim. Unpublished Dmin Thesis

Foster, Tim. 2014. *The Suburban Captivity of the Church.* Brookvale, Sydney: Acorn Press.

Frost, Michael. 2006. *Exiles: Living Missionally in a Post-Christian Culture.* Peabody, MA: Hendrickson Publishers.

Frost, Michael & Hirsch, Alan. 2003. *The Shaping of Things to Come: Innovation and Mission for the 21st Century Church.* Peabody, MA: Hendrickson Publishers.

Gibbs, Eddie. 2013. *Rebirth of the Church: Applying Paul's Vision for Ministry in Our Post-Christian World.* Baker Academic.

Gibbs, Eddie & Bolger Ryan K. 2005. *Emerging Churches: Creating Christian Community in Postmodern Cultures.* Grand Rapids, MI: Baker.

Goheen, Michael W. 2011. *A Light to the Nations: The Missional Church and the Biblical Story.* Grand Rapids, MI: Baker.

Green, Joel B. 2004. "Faithful Witness in the Diaspora: The Holy Spirit and the exiled people of God according to 1 Peter", *The Holy Spirit in Christian Origins: Essays in Honour of James D. G. Dunn,* edited by James D. G. Dunn et. al., 282-295. Grand Rapids, MI: Eerdmans.

———. 2007. "Living as Exiles: The Church in the Diaspora in 1 Peter". In *Holiness and Ecclesiology in the New Testament,* edited by Kent E. Brower and Andy Johnson, 311-325. Grand Rapids, MI: Eerdmans.

Guba, E., & Lincoln, Y. 1994. Competing Paradigms in Qualitative Research. Quoted in Carol A. Bailey *A Guide to Qualitative Field Research.* 2nd ed. (Thousand Oaks, CA: Pine Forge, 2007).

Guder, Darrell, L. 1998. *Missional Church: A Vision for the Sending of the Church in North America.* Grand Rapids, MI: Eerdmans.

———. 2007. *The Continuing Conversion of the Church.* Grand Rapids, MI: Eerdmans.

Gustafson, David M. 2018. *Gospel Witness: Evangelism in Word and Deed*. Grand Rapids, MI: Eerdmans.

Hartung Blake. 2017. "Back to the Future: Faithful Presence in a non-Christian world." *Modern Reformation*. 26, no. 6 (Nov-Dec):

Hiebert, Paul G. 1983. *Cultural Anthropology* 2nd ed. Grand Rapids, Mich: Baker Book House.

Hirsch, Alan. 2006. *The Forgotten Ways: Reactivating the Missional Church*. Grand Rapids, MI: Baker. Kindle.

_____, Alan. 2009. *The Forgotten Ways Handbook: A Practical Guide for Developing Missional Churches*. Grand Rapids, MI: Baker.

Hunsberger, George R. & Van Gelder, Craig. 1996. *The Church Between Gospel and Culture: The Emerging Mission in North America*. Grand Rapids, MI: Eerdmans.

Hunter, James Davison. 2010. *To Change the World: The Irony, Tragedy, and Possibility of Christianity in the Late Modern World*. New York, NY: Oxford University Press.

Jensen, Phillip, D. "What is Church for?" *The Briefing*, 397 (Jan-Feb): 14-21.

Jobes, Karin H. 2005 *1 Peter*. Grand Rapids, MI: Baker Academic.

Judd, S. & Cable, Kenneth. 1987. *Sydney Anglicans: A History of the Diocese*. AIO: Sydney.

Kang, Steven, S. "Introduction to the Special Focus: Ministry with Emerging Generations in a Post-Christian World." *Christian Education Journal*, 3, 8, no. 2 (2011): 326-30.

Keller, Timothy, J. 2001 "Missional Church,". http://www.redeemer2.com/resources/papers/missional.pdf.

_____. 2012. *Center Church: Doing Balanced, Gospel-Centered Ministry in Your City*. Zondervan.

_____. 2020. "How to Reach the West (Again)." The Gospel Coalition, March 12, 2020. Accessed August 25, 2020. https://www.thegospelcoalition.org/article/how-to-reach-the-west-again/.

Knox, D. Broughton. 1986. "The Biblical Concept of Fellowship." In *Selected Works Vol. II: Church and Ministry*, edited by Kirsten Birkett. 3 vols. Kingsford, NSW: Matthias Media.

Kostenberger A. J. & O'Brien, Peter, T. 2001 *Salvation to the Ends of the Earth: A Biblical Theology of Mission*. Downers Grove: IVP.

Kuhn, Chase R., 2017. *The Ecclesiology of Donald Robinson and D. Broughton Knox: Exposition, Analysis, and Theological Evaluation*. Eugene, OR: Wipf and Stock.

Kreminski, Karina. 2018. *Urban Spirituality: Embracing God's Mission in the Neighbourhood*. Skyforest, CA: Urban Loft.

Lette, Kathy & Carey, Gabrielle. 1979. *Puberty Blues*. Carlton, VIC: McPhee Gribble.

Lewis, C. S. 1942. The Weight of Glory *Theology http://www.wheelersburg.net/Downloads/Lewis%20Glory.pdf* accessed 22/9/2020

Mackay, Hugh. 1993. *Reinventing Australia: The Mind and Mood of Australia in the 90s*

_____. 2010. *What Makes us Tick? The Ten Desires that Drive us*. Sydney, NSW: Hachette.

_____. 2016. *Beyond Belief: How We Find Meaning, with or without Religion*. Sydney: Macmillan.

McAlpine, Stephen. 2017. "The Slippery Slope was a Precipice After All" https://stephenmcalpine.com/the-slippery-slope-was-a-precipice-after-all/.

McCrindle Research 2017. *Faith and Belief in Australia*. Baulkham Hills: McCrindle Research. Accessed May 5, 2020. https://2qean3b1jjd1s8781200l5ji-wpengine.netdna-ssl.com/wp-content/uploads/2018/04/Faith-and-Belief-in-Australia-Report_McCrindle_2017.pdf.

Michaels, J. Ramsey. 1988. *1 Peter*. Word Biblical Commentary 49. Nashville, TN: Thomas Nelson.

Morris, Leon. 1992. *The Gospel According to Matthew*. Grand Rapids: Eerdmans.

Murray, Stuart. 2004. *Post-Christendom: Church and Mission in a Strange New World*. Milton Keyes, UK: Paternoster.

Newbigin, Lesslie. 1963. "Developments During 1962 – An Editorial Survey." *International Review of Mission* 100, no. 2 (November): 391-401.

———, Lesslie. 1986. *Foolishness to the Greeks: the Gospel and Western Culture*. Grand Rapids, MI: Eerdmans.

———, Lesslie. 1987. "Evangelism in the City." *Reformed Review* 41, no. 1 (Autumn): 3-8.

———, Lesslie. 1989. *The Gospel in a Pluralist Society*. Grand Rapids, MI: Eerdmans.

———, Lesslie. 1995. *The Open Secret: An Introduction to the Theology of Mission*. Grand Rapids, MI: Eerdmans.

Niebuhr, H. Richard. 1951. *Christ and Culture*. New York, NY: HarperCollins.

Nikolajsen, Jeppe. 2013 "Missional Church: A Historical and Theological Analysis of an Ecclesiological Tradition." *International Review of Mission* 102, no. 397 (November): 249-61.

———, Jeppe. 2012. "Beyond Christendom: Lesslie Newbigin as a Post-Christendom Theologian." *Exchange* 41: 364-380.

O'Donovan, Oliver. 1996. *The Desire of the Nations*

Oldenburg, Ray. 1989. *The Great Good Place: Cafes, Coffee Shops, Bookstores, Bars, Hair Salons, and Other Hangouts at the Heart of a Community*. Boston, MA: Da Capo Press.

Patton Michael. 1990. *Qualitative Evaluation and Research Methods*. Newbury Park: Sage Publications.

Payne, Tony, and Colin Marshall. 2009. *The Trellis and the Vine*. Kingsford, NSW: St Matthias Press.

Piper, John. 1995. *Future Grace*. Leicester, UK: IVP.

Priest, Robert J. "Experience-near theologizing" in Diverse Human Contexts" in *Globalizing Theology: Belief and Practice in an Era of World Christianity*, Craig Ott & Harold A. Netland (eds), (Grand Rapids: Baker Academic, 2006).

Rayner, Keith. 2006. Interview by Rachael Kohn. *ABC Faith in the Fifties*, September 24. Accessed October 23, 2020. https://www.abc.net.au/radionational/programs/archived/spiritofthings/faith-in-the-fifties/3348018.

Religious Affiliation in Australia. https://www.abs.gov.au/articles/religious-affiliation-australia

Reyne, James. *Heaven on a Stick*. Recorded 1987. Capitol Records, EMI.

Robinson, Donald, W. B. 1974 "The Doctrine of the church and its Implications for Evangelism". *Interchange* 15 (1974): 156-62. Reprinted in *Donald Robinson: Selected Works*. Edited by Peter G. Bolt and Mark D. Thompson. 2008. Vol 2, *Preaching God's Word*. Camperdown, NSW: Australian Church Record. 2:103-113.

Sayers, Mark. 2016. *Disappearing Church: From Cultural Relevance to Gospel Resilience*. Chicago, IL: Moody Publishers.

Seland, Torrey. 2009. "Resident Aliens in Mission: Missional Practices in the Emerging Church of 1 Peter." *Bulletin for Biblical Research* 19 (4): 565-598.

Shaw, R. Daniel. 1990. "Culture and Evangelism: A Model for Missiological Strategy." *Missiology: An International Review* XVIII, no. 3 (July): 291-304.

Sheridan, Greg. 2016. "Christian Churches Drifting Too far from the Marketplace of Ideas." *Australian*, June 4, 2016. Opinion.

Sheridan, Greg. 2018. *God is Good for You: A Defence of Christianity in Troubled Times.* Crows Nest, NSW: Allen & Unwin.

Smith, James, K. A. 2016. *You Are What You Love: The Spiritual power of Habit.* Grand Rapids: MI: Baker.

———, James, K. A. 2009. *Desiring the Kingdom: Worship, Worldview, and Cultural Formation.* Cultural Liturgies, vol. 1. Grand Rapids: Baker Academic.

———, James, K. A. 2017. *Awaiting the King: Reforming Public Theology.* Grand Rapids, MI: Baker Academic.

Smith-Christopher, Daniel L. 2002. *A Biblical Theology of Exile.* Minneapolis: Fortress Press.

Stallard, Mike. 2015. "Post-Christian Culture as an Aid to Ministry." *Journal of Ministry and Theology.* 19 Issue 1 (Spring): 59-81.

Sutherland, Martin. 2005. "The Kingdom made Visible: a Missional Theology of Church." *Stimulus.* 13 no. 1 (Feb): 2-7.

Timmis, Steve, and Tim Chester. 2012. *Everyday Church: Gospel Communities on Mission.* Wheaton, IL: Crossway.

———. *Total Church: A Radical Reshaping around Gospel Community.* Nottingham, UK: Intervarsity Press, 2007.

Vandervelde, George. 1996. "The Church as Missionary Community: The Church as Central Disclosure Point of the Kingdom", unpublished paper. Quoted in J. B. Nikolajsen 2012. "Beyond Christendom: Lesslie Newbigin as a Post-Christendom Theologian." *Exchange* 41: 364-380.

Van Gelder, Craig. 2000. *The Essence of the Church: a Community Created by the Spirit.* Grand Rapids, MI: Baker.

Van Gelder, Craig, and Zscheile, Dwight J. 2011. *The Missional Church in Perspective: Mapping Trends and Shaping the Conversation.* Grand Rapids, MI: Baker Academic.

Vanhoozer, Kevin, J. 2007. *Everyday Theology: How to Read Cultural Texts and Interpret Trends.* Grand Rapids, MI: Baker Academic

Veith, Gene Edward. 2020. *Post Christian: a Guide to Contemporary Thought and Culture.* Wheaton: Crossway.

Volf, Miroslav. 1994. "Soft Difference: Theological Reflections on the Relation between Church and Culture in 1 Peter." *Ex Auditu* 10 (January): 15-30.

Williams, Roy. 2015. *Post-God Nation? How religion fell off the radar in Australia – and what might be done to get it back on.* Sydney: Harper Collins.

Wright, Christopher, J. H. 2006. *The Mission of God: Unlocking the Bible's Grand Narrative.* Downers Grove: InterVarsity Press.

———, Christoper, J.H. "Truth with a Mission: Reading All Scripture Missiologically." 2011. SBJT 15, no. 2: 4-15.